My Life
as
George
Johanson

by George Johanson

George Johanson

Portland, Oregon

My Life as George Johanson

ISBN: 978-0-692-18277-2

Copyright 2018, all rights George Johanson

www.johansonfinearts.com

Photo credits

All photos are by family members or unknown, except the following:
Don Normark, pgs. 15, 33, 34, 38, 58, 65, 100, 104, 112, 113, 114,
Gerald Robinson, pg. 24, The Oregonian, pg. 148, Steve Anchell, pg. 177,
Manson Kennedy, pg. 184.
Courtesy of Pacific Northwest College of Art Albert Solheim Library
Archives, images on pgs. 22, 28.

Many thanks to Mollie Gregory, Van Le, Edwina Norton and Linny Stovall
for their invaluable help in reading the manuscript, making suggestions and
editing.

All artworks are by George Johanson except as otherwise indicated.
Printed: Symbiosis Printing
Design: Emerson Creative

Cover image: "Bridge and Fire," acrylic, 1981
Back cover image: "Self Portrait," pencil & wash, 1977

For Phyllis, who made me a
more complete person

Contents

Foreward

I started this memoir last year, after my wife Phyllis passed away. This has been a time of introspection for me, of mulling things over, of adding things up. I decided I needed to write about my life, to figure out for myself what it has meant. I made a list of events and points of interest going back to my earliest memories, then proceeded to flesh them out.

It's impossible to write about everything. Inevitably, a lot is left out. It's not my intention to include or exclude any of my friends. I love them all. Those who appear in the book are there because they are part of particular events.

This book tells the story of myself and of the art communities of Portland, New York and London, as I experienced them.

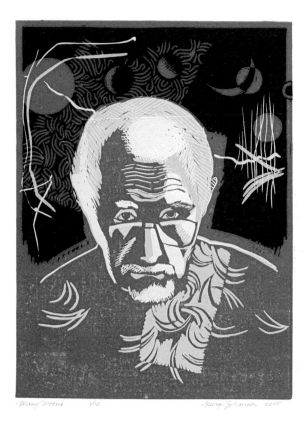

"Many Moons," self portrait, linocut, 2015

Introduction

There should be a rule that you are not allowed to depart this world without first writing an essay, or at least a few paragraphs, on what life was all about for you. Some kind of summing up. What did it mean to be here in this world?

For me, the answer revolves around being an artist. The most important part of being an artist is to take a long, hard look at the world. What does it really look like? And what does it feel like? In doing that, you may discover, bit by bit, something about who you are as an individual. And that process is never finished. "Please Lord," said Hokusai when he was on his death bed, "give me just one more day to make one last drawing."

Art keeps me going. The possibility of new discoveries. Even after decades of making images, I still have the desire to make one more drawing or combination of colors or forms that I haven't yet tried.

I paint, therefore I am. Making art as a proof of being. Could be true. Here is my attempt to see if I can make some sense of who, and where, and why I am.

Me at two years, nine months, 1931

Chapter One

Childhood and Adolescence

My mother's parents were immigrants from Finland. My father's were immigrants from Sweden. I was born in Seattle in 1928, only ten years after the First World War ended, and one year before the stock market crash that precipitated the great Depression. That latter event helped form the person I am, and in many deep ways.

Frankenstein

Movies were the main source of entertainment during the Depression. Everyone went to the movies at least once a week. Admission was cheap, 15 cents for the neighborhood theaters. There wasn't anything like an age rating for films, and my folks couldn't afford a baby sitter, so my sister Marianne and I accompanied our folks to whatever movie they wanted to see. Many were not appropriate for young kids. Many films of the time were noir, with very dark themes. Frankenstein was one of those films that scared me a lot. For weeks afterwards I would lie awake imagining the monster coming down the street toward our house looking for me. It was personal, and very scary.

At a very early age I had a habit of sleep walking. My mother would wake up to find me standing at the foot of their bed, just staring at her and my father. She said it frightened her, as I'm sure it would have. But I have no direct memory of that sleep walking.

The Kids Are Missing

We lived in Seattle on 24th Avenue NW, several blocks North of Market Street. Late one night when I was not quite 5 and my kid sister not quite 3, my Dad was at the neighborhood tavern drinking up his meager paycheck. It was about 11 p.m. and my Mom decided she had to get Dad and bring him back home. The tavern was not too far from the house, so she took a chance and left my sister and me sound asleep and went to get him. She was gone only a short time, but I woke up and found the house empty. So I did the logical thing that a 5 year old would do. I woke up my sister. We put on our bathrobes and slippers and went out looking for Mom. We plodded along down toward Market St because I knew where the Bagdad movie theater was. I wonder how many people saw two little kids in their bathrobes walking along the street late at night. Finally, some people coming out of the movie theater asked us where our parents were and where we were going. They found a policeman and turned us over to him. He led us by the hands to the police station in Ballard.

Meanwhile, my folks had returned home to find our beds empty. Imagine how frantic they were! Kidnapped, is the only thing they must have been thinking. By the time they located us some time later we were sitting at the Police station eating ice cream. I still remember seeing them come through the doors of the station. We all burst out crying. Probably the police did too. That event must have been the most terrifying moments of my young parents' lives.

Alcoholism

In the early years, my father drank. In fact he was a falling-down-drunk alcoholic. He lost several jobs because of it. And on many occasions I was mortified when he showed up drunk at the playground to insist, for no reason, that I had to go home. At other times I had to help my mother drag him up off the floor and into bed. Alcoholism ran in his family. His father, his brother and one of his sisters were all alcoholics.

The Cure

When I was about 8, my mother was at the end of her rope about the drinking and made my Dad move out. The separation lasted about a year and a half. The prospect of losing his family finally brought him to the point where he knew he had to stop drinking. He checked himself into a sanitarium that specialized in curing alcoholism. Their method was to offer the patient any drink he wanted. They had a cabinet full of beer, wine, vodka, scotch, bourbon, and other booze. The catch was that first he had to swallow some medicine that later reacted with the booze, and produced violent nausea. The idea was to repeat this procedure until just the mere sight of the bottles would provoke that negative reaction. He was there for some weeks. And it worked. That was the end of his drinking.

Mom had been working in a delicatessen to support us kids

Mom, Marianne, Dad, me, 1937

and she had sitter help from an aunt. After my mother became convinced that Dad's sobriety was for good, she took him back and we became a family again. He never returned to drinking.

In later years, when the family and friends got together for cards, he would sometimes fill a one ounce shot glass with beer and nurse that one tiny amount for a couple of hours. At first we were leery of it. Was this a slippery slope? Would he slip back into the old habits? But it never went beyond that one shot glass full of beer. His drinking days were indeed over. This was long before Alcoholics Anonymous. Given what a total grip the alcoholism had had on him, I am amazed at how thoroughly he finally overcame it. I have to think that underneath, somewhere, was a well of willpower that he was able to call upon. It is as if I had two fathers. The one who drank, and the later one who was sober.

The Depression

That was a hard but interesting time to grow up in. We were poor, as were all the kids I played with. There were exceptions. When I went to the house of a better off kid, I was aware that they had things that the rest of us didn't. For instance, Delicious apples. Those were more expensive than other varieties of apple so we never had them at home. They were much tastier than today's Delicious and were a special treat. I was quite aware of being poor, and I felt a lot of embarrassment being forced to stand in long lines with my mother and sister when the government was doling out free clothing.

Dad was a produce grocer when he had work, and he was quite good at writing signs for the store and turned them out with a lot of flourish. He had only an 8th grade education, but he had a talent for numbers. He could calculate columns of large numbers in his head faster than I could add them up with paper and pencil. This ability helped make him a very good poker player and good at handicapping horses. After he stopped drinking he brought home

Pencil drawing, age 10, 1938

a small but steady amount of money from both the card rooms in downtown Seattle and the race track. He would carefully and thoroughly analyze the dope sheet on the horses and make shrewd guesses about which horses were "ready." And then he'd bet small amounts and never take wild chances.

Freedom

In those days parents didn't feel the need to constantly monitor the kids' whereabouts. On weekends and after school, we had complete freedom to make our own fun and to just show up at the end of the day for supper.

Between our house and Ballard Beach were woods that gave us a great area to play in and invent activities. We got a pulley, put up a long rope and set up a zip line between trees and across a deep gully. Great fun. There were many kids in neighboring blocks where we lived, so we could play endless games of hide-and-seek, sand lot baseball, and one game I found was lots of fun: tossing a tennis ball all the way over a two story house to players on the other side. It was exhilarating to see how far the ball flew, and to watch it return back at you over the roof.

I was named after my Dad (with the customary Swedish two middle names) George Eugene Ernest Johanson, Jr. I was called Junior around the house and when my Mom called me to supper. Other kids mocked me until I eventually asked Mom to drop the "Junior" and to please call me George. Which, after that, she did. To my great relief.

Movies

Movies were the poor people's main entertainment. The Ballard district had two movie theaters, The Roxy and the Bagdad. Both showed second-run movies, usually about twelve months after the more expensive first run in theaters in downtown Seattle. Admission was about 15 cents for two features plus a cartoon

(Loony Tunes, Popeye, Bugs Bunny) and a newsreel called "The March of Time." Saturday matinees always provided a serial, Flash Gordon or The Lone Ranger. The serials were about 20 minutes long, ending in a cliff hanger to bring us back the next week.

At the Roxy, Wednesday was Dime Night. For 10 cents you got the usual double bill plus a free dinner plate of clear glass. While you were watching the movies, the plate would be perched on your lap. Many nights brought the sudden crash of a plate falling and breaking, followed by hooting from the audience. What togetherness!

Magic

Like many kids before and since I loved magic tricks, and I loved learning how to do them, something I have not outgrown. For my part I have always felt that the evocative qualities in art, the illusion in it, is rather like the production of an illusion in magic. At any rate, my fascination with the illusion in a good magic trick continues. I can often figure out how the magic was probably done. When I can't, I don't always want to know.

Swimming with Turds

I loved to swim. My mother and my aunt or others would take my sister and me for a picnic to Golden Gardens or Ballard Beach. The salt water was very chilly, even in summer. We had to steel ourselves to get into it. It was not too bad after you got used to it. At Golden Gardens the water was very clear and we could see the tiny crabs clambering about on the bottom. We could also

Self portrait, pencil drawing, age 10, 1938

see very clearly the sudden drop off that we needed to avoid. At Ballard Beach the conditions were a little different. No drop off, but the swimming area was near a sewer outlet. And as disgusting as it sounds, you had to push little remnants of turds aside as you swam. We just accepted it. Environmental awareness was a long way in the future.

Smells

Smells are such a strong memory trigger. When I was very

young the afternoon paper would arrive and I would sprawl out on the living room floor to read the funnies with my nose just inches above the paper. There is a certain smell to newspaper ink that, for many years later, evoked powerful memories of that particular paper-reading time. In recent years, the composition of the ink has changed and that special smell with its particular trigger is no more.

Rabies

One day when I was about 8, I was playing by the railroad tracks with some friends when we came upon a stray dog. He was a smallish gray wire-haired dog. He seemed agitated, and when I was trying to pet him he bit me on the ankle and then ran off. The wound was deep, but it healed over. A couple of days later my parents began to worry that the dog may have been rabid. My Mom took me to a clinic and the doctor decided that the wound needed to be cleaned out. I don't know why, but there was no anesthetic. He took a scalpel and sliced through the skin that had grown over the wound and then proceeded to cauterize it by jamming an acid filled tube into it. My mother held onto me tightly as I screamed my lungs out. It hurt like hell, but it must have been even worse for my poor mother, having to endure my screams.

What followed was also something to endure. For a period of two weeks I had to go daily to have a long needle thrust into my stomach injecting some kind of serum. The injection treatment was twice a day for the first week, and once a day for the next week. Such was the treatment for fending off rabies. At least it worked, and I survived, both the bite and the needle.

Drawing

I started drawing before my earliest memories. Drawing was fun, because moving a pencil around on a piece of paper could magically make something appear in three dimensions. For me, that sorcery in art keeps it compelling. My parents and my teachers were wonderfully encouraging from the beginning. My fourth grade teacher took me aside after class one day and told me I should set my sights on magazine illustration. That particular moment is bright in my memory, and from then on, I had a singular goal. I had no hesitation about what occupation I would pursue in life. (I did, however, later, change focus away from commercial art.)

Daisy Mae Naked

For their part, my folks were more than encouraging. They were always hauling out my sketches to show visitors. This was very flattering and fine with me. Although one day, to my embarrassment, they found among my drawings one I had done from the Lil Abner comic strip; I had redrawn Daisy Mae nude with a little tiny branch of a tree just covering her pubic area. I was about 11 years old, and mortified. My folks and the visitors were in good spirits and jokingly remarked how fortunate it was that the tree limb happened to be there. I endured the jokes and thereafter I securely hid any such drawings.

Copying Movie Ads

When I was a kid, movies were in black and white and because of the noir nature of the stories, the emphasis was on sharp contrasts of dark and light. This was reflected in the movie ads as they appeared in the newspaper. Sharp contrasts of shadow and light on the figures produced dramatic effects. I was very attracted to the patterning. I made lots of copies of the faces in the ads, and I learned a great deal from them. Much later in art school, I began to study cubism and found similar concerns in the cubists' emphasis on flat shapes. That early exposure to finding the relationship of shape to shape is still the basis of much of what I do in drawing and painting.

Salmon Fishing

My Dad and I often went fishing together. This involved getting up at 4 a.m. and going down to the Ballard boat docks where we would rent a row boat (sometimes with an outboard motor) before dawn and row or motor out onto the Sound along with dozens of other small boats. It was marvelously quiet. The water was often glassy smooth, and we could hear the faint sound of the other fishermen talking in low voices in the distance. We'd go out a long way and then slowly troll. Sometimes we caught a salmon. Then we'd bring it back to the dock and clean it. Often we'd get "skunked." But when we did get a fish, we would sometimes put on long faces and pretend to my Mom that we had had no luck. This was particularly fun on the rare day when we brought home a really big one of 20 pounds or more.

Don

Don Normark and I were the same age and first met when we were just starting the 7th grade at Seattle's John Marshall Junior High School. We were two little blonde 12-year-old Swedish boys and both terribly shy. At recess on one of the first days of school we were standing outside watching the other kids at play. I felt sorry for Don, and as I found out later, he felt sorry for me. So we struck up a conversation, and that was the beginning of a friendship that became very close and lasted some 74 years till his death in 2014.

We did a lot of things together and had many boyhood adventures. We made our first long camping trip at age 14. We loaded our gear on the back of our bicycles, took the ferry from Seattle across Puget Sound to Port Angeles, rode the bikes and then pushed them 5 miles or so up into the Olympic National Park to the Elwha Campground. We had a small tent, cooking utensils, fishing rods and our bows. It was an idyllic week. The only thing was, we weren't any good at catching fish. The stream was shallow in places and loaded with trout. But we had no luck catching them. We tried shooting them with our bows and arrows, but the water changed the angle as the arrow went in the water and we would miss every time. We did have a couple of delicious fish dinners thanks to the generosity of a family camping near us whose father was a more accomplished fisherman than we were. We had to eat with towels placed over our heads forming tents over our plates to fend off the hornets who were after our meal.

At the end of the week we got on our bikes and had a fast 5 mile ride down the mountain on our way back. How exhilarating that was! The next day after returning home my bike frame

Don on left, me on right, when we were 13, 1941

snapped off right under the handle bars. If that had happened on our fast joyful ride down the long mountain road…!

Making a Bomb

It is a wonder we arrived at adulthood with limbs and eyes in working order. One day we decided it would be interesting to make a bomb. At least what we thought would be some kind of a Molotov cocktail. We filled a glass milk bottle with gasoline and

Don on left, me on right, when we were 18, 1946

put a top on it. We thought it would be prudent to take it out of the city to the countryside to blow it up. We had no car, so we hitchhiked, got a ride with two ladies, and sat in the back seat with our device in a paper bag. One of them said, "I think I smell gasoline." I don't remember what we said in return, but they did eventually deliver us to some site far beyond the city limits where we set up our "bomb" in the dirt of a vacant piece of land. Home made bombs were in the news because of the Russo-Finnish war where the Finns made a simple device out of a gasoline container with a fuse that they used against Russian tanks. The Molotov cocktail.

We half buried the bottle and inserted a rag in the opening, lit it, and ran back to a safe distance. Nothing. After several futile attempts, we gave up. The enemy tanks would have been quite safe from us. But we did have success in a real sense. We returned to Seattle with all our limbs intact.

High School Art

I attended Roosevelt High School where the art classes were not very good at that time. I learned nothing solid about art or about art history. But I did paint lots of posters for school events, such as dances. Often I did posters depicting a pretty girl with large pointed breasts (my ideal, and also the fashion at the time). Sometimes they would be censored by someone in authority, adding some paint to reduce the size of the breasts. I was disgruntled about it, too shy to voice an objection.

War

We heard the news about Pearl Harbor when Don and I were coming out of a movie on Sunday afternoon on December 7th, 1941. We saw newspaper "extras" in the boxes with huge headlines "War with Japan." It was shocking, scary, and exciting, all at once. Don and I were 13, so the war would dominate the background and the foreground of the next four years of high school. Everything changed. Life and society shifted gears overnight. But for me and my friends there was not much thought about actually being called up. We were too young. We did, though, get involved in the

Civil Defense and other homeland wartime activities.

Almost immediately there began to be plenty of jobs. My Dad went to work in the ship yards. Don and I had a variety of part time and summer jobs during those years. I worked in the A&P grocery on Saturdays, mostly bagging groceries. I was quite good at judging the available spaces in the bag. I was very efficient and all the checkers wanted me for their bagger. Judging how an object will fit into a space is still something I am good at. Maybe I should go back to a bagging job some day.

Since Don and I applied for a number of summer jobs together, we often found jobs at the same place. Off-bearing a ripping machine, (pulling away and stacking the sawn boards) at one of the local lumber mills was one of my jobs. Don and I would play tag at lunch hour on the log booms floating in the mill pond, leaping from one to the other, trying not to slip off into the water.

Another summer job was baling bags in a paper mill. That machine had a flat metal plate that came down with a lot of force to squeeze the bags together for baling with a length of wire. One time, when I was reaching inside to retrieve the end of the wire, the lever got tripped and it came down on my arm. Luckily there were bags in place that cushioned the blow and my arm was in such a position that it just got squeezed hard and bruised but didn't break.

Those factory jobs gave me a real appreciation for the mind-numbing nature of repetitive jobs and an appreciation for how terribly long eight hours of work can seem. I would look far up near the ceiling to see the small dirty windows of the factory and think about how many more weeks it would be before the job ended and I could get in some summer camping.

One summer job was lots of fun. Don and I were both hired to be assistants to a surveyor at Sand Point Naval Air Station for a couple of months. The work was very relaxed, and we got to be outside in the fresh air and sun. And we got to watch the Navy sea planes landing and taking off.

Somebody Else's Girl

When I was about 14, the family rented out one of our rooms to a young lady. She was 18, very pretty and buxom, and the newly married wife of a sailor who was away on duty. My own sleeping arrangement at the time was a bed in one corner of our large living room. A curtain strung across it give my space some privacy. On Sundays, I would get the papers and take the funnies back to my bed to read. The young lady, still in her pajamas, would come behind the curtain to read the funnies too, and in order to "see better" she lay down on top of me (both of us facing downward). That's all that happened with the funny paper reading. But I did look forward to those Sunday mornings.

Burlesque

Don and I discovered burlesque at the Rivoli Theater in downtown Seattle. At the tail end of the burlesque era, the Rivoli was one of the last of the burlesque houses still on the circuit. We didn't know or care much about the great burlesque tradition. We were interested in the strip tease acts. The Rivoli showed movies as well. First came the movie, then the lights would come up and the live performance would commence. These included several acts, like juggling, some slapstick and very raunchy skits, and finally the star stripper, always performing with a live band. Colored lights played on the stage. We saw the likes of Blaze Starr, Lillie St Cyr and Sally Rand. They would strip down to a G string and nipple stick ons. It was strip tease with the emphasis on "tease." For two teenage boys it was very titillating.

You were supposed to be 18 to buy a ticket. We were a couple of years younger than that requirement, but enforcement of those laws was very lax. Of course we didn't want to admit to our parents where we were going, so we always picked out a legitimate movie that we were supposed to be going to, then made up a plausible story about it. How devious.

Uncensored Sex

During the 1940s in Seattle high schools, very few students had any real experience about sex, beyond petting. The vast majority left high school as virginal as when they entered. One summer in 1943, Don and I were hitchhiking in Eastern Washington, picking fruit and seeing the sights (Grand Coulee Dam, for instance). We found out that the new Jane Russell film "The Outlaw" was playing in Ellensburg. It had been banned in Seattle and most of the rest of Washington State, thanks to the scene depicting the heroine climbing into bed with the wounded cowboy "to keep him warm." The film was also reputed to show plenty of cleavage. Ellensburg was about 60 miles off the route we had planned, but what was 60 miles when compared to the possibility of seeing such an edifying film?

Howard Hughes was backing the film. The advertising for it in

Ellensburg included a sky-writing plane spelling out "The Outlaw" and then drawing two large circles.

The crucial scene did expose her breasts somewhat (not the nipples), but as with the burlesque strippers, if you told yourself that what you were watching was illicit, it made it more exciting. The film was, needless to say, very innocent by today's standards. But at the time, it seemed to us all that extra travel was worth it.

Sports

In high school, I ran high hurdles for the track team. Don and I looked a lot alike, since we were both blonde Swedish boys. At one big track meet I was poised on the starting line when I heard from the stands, "Come on Normark!" I gave it my best, but Don didn't win that day.

Archery

We took up archery in a serious way. We often practiced shooting where we shouldn't have, like at Green Lake Park on winter days when not too many people were around. We sometimes tried to see how far we could shoot, and I shudder to think of what might have happened if someone had suddenly appeared underneath our arcing arrows.

We went deer hunting once during the bow hunting season. I did get one shot at a deer at fairly close range, but he was standing in a thicket of reedy branches, and an arrow is easily sent off course if it hits something like a reed. At the time, I was disappointed by the miss. Now of course I'm glad I didn't hit it, and I would never

"Carol," pencil, 1947

think of going hunting again.

Carol

When I was 14, my second sister, Carol, was born. Don and I rode our bikes out to the hospital to see her and visit Mom, but we were turned away. Since we were still kids ourselves there was too much chance for us to bring along unwanted viruses.

Later I spent lots of time drawing my new baby sister. And in Carol's first years my sister Marianne and I would take her to the park in a stroller. On several occasions passers-by would assume we were the parents, and since we were about 16 and 14 at the time, we passed by many raised eyebrows and disapproving glances. We were amused by that.

The Museum Art School, corner of SW Madison and 10th, 1946

Chapter Two

Museum Art School

At the end of my high school year, in 1946, I received a scholarship from Scholastic Magazine to attend the Museum Art School in Portland. Don had set off to join the Marines. The war was over. He was joining to take advantage of the GI Bill. My scholarship was full tuition for the school year. I was very cocky. I considered that the school was lucky that I was allowing them to give me tuition. I had a lot of pride in my drawing abilities, but I had no idea how much I didn't know. In a very short time, I realized that I had a lot to learn.

Louie Bunce was the first faculty member I met when Dean Bill Givler showed me around the art school a week before classes started. I was still 17, Louie was 39. The word charismatic was invented for people like Louie. On being introduced, he offered his hand. This doesn't seem unusual now. Back then few adults would offer to shake hands with a kid. But it was a gesture of respect that was genuine. He was a wonderful painter himself and he was excited by the potentialities of his students and what they might become.

Other instructors at the school were also very strong and dedicated artists, as well as enthusiastic teachers. Besides Louie, the other instructor who I became very close to was Jack McLarty. Jack

Louie Bunce, 1948

was only 9 years older than I, but had had a lot of life experiences, and his art had already developed an original style.

The Museum Art School had many excellent teachers. A lot of credit goes to the Dean, Bill Givler, a very good painter and printmaker himself who personally chose all of the faculty. Back then there was no faculty council and no school committees. Bill had the highest standards and was looking for excellent artists who could teach. The first criterion was the quality of their work. Very few had a degree. Mike Russo was one of the few who had one, having graduated from Yale. Mike taught art history as well as other classes. His art history classes were great. They were more than just looking at styles and memorizing dates. He made them alive and engaging as he related the art of an era to its politics and social structure. When Don came to visit me in Portland, I took him to sit in on Mike's class just because I knew he would find it so interesting.

The School's building was attached to the side of the museum. It was built on the foundation of an old grade school and consisted of six large studios with skylights. The studios had wooden floors. Many faculty members as well as students smoked. I was a school janitor and swept up after morning classes as well as after school, and always there were tons of cigarette butts. Given that we used a lot of turpentine and other solvents, why didn't the whole thing just go up in flames?

The entrance to the School was through the front doors of the museum. Many first rate shows came to the museum, and the students had a great deal of access to the exhibitions during regular hours, as well as with their instructors at other times.

In that year of 1946, the Museum Art School suddenly doubled its enrollment over previous years, thanks to returning GIs who were making use of the GI Bill. The School was still small, about 85 students total. The small size meant that we had plenty of personal attention from the instructors. The School had an intimate quality that felt like teachers and students were all learning together. And this carried over to after school life such as parties and friendships with instructors. It was all very serious study and serious fun too.

I became close friends with Rick Norwood and Jack Hammack. Both of them were returning GIs and talented students. The three of us would meet Louie after his night class at 10 p.m. and

Green Spot Tavern mural sketch, Louie Bunce, 1947

go to a tavern and drink beer until the tavern closed at 1. Though I was 18 by that time, the legal drinking age was still 21, as it is now. But I don't remember ever being asked for ID. The laws about such things were not so strictly enforced back then.

Tavern Mural

The "Green Spot," a tavern a dozen blocks from the school was a favorite of ours, and we got to know the owner quite well. She was agreeable to a proposal we made to paint a mural on one long interior wall in exchange for free beer for the year. Each of us drew up a sketch and then when we compared them we all agreed Louie's was the best. The plan was to work on the mural together, following his sketch. Unfortunately by the time we were ready to show the sketch, the tavern had been sold and the new owner wasn't interested in a mural. So the deal fell through. But Louie's handsome sketch is still around and hangs happily on my living room wall.

That first year Jack McLarty was my life drawing teacher. Though he was a strong and confident teacher, he had a very soft voice and I had to strain to understand him as he gave his introductory talk.

He was a big influence on me, both artistically and politically. He had very strong pacifist ideas and we talked about pacifism a lot. When it came time for me to register for the draft, I told the draft board I wanted to register as a conscientious objector, and since there was no war going on at that time (1947) they issued me a draft card with 4E status: exempt as a conscientious objector. No hearing. They just issued me the card. This status was good until my wallet was stolen 3 years later. More on this to come.

Changing Course

When I entered the Museum Art School I had ambitions to be a commercial illustrator. By the end of the first semester I had been exposed to a world of art I hadn't known existed. My notion of what I wanted to do with my life had changed dramatically, and when I went back to Seattle to see my parents at Christmas break, I announced that I had given up commercial art and was going to become a painter. They were set back on their heels. "If that's what you want, OK, but realize that you can't count on us for a living." I did realize that, and assured them I would make it on my own. I must say that given their background of poverty and struggles during the depression, they took it very well.

The McLartys had a large house on NW Overton and 23rd (in what later became the Pearl District) where they rented out four of the upstairs rooms to lodgers. During my second year at the school, I rented one of the rooms. Jack gave me a lift to school sometimes or I walked. During that time the Pearl district was made up entirely of warehouses, machine shops and other grungy

At the Museum Art School, 1948. Top from left: Rick Norwood, Jack
Hammack, Manuel Izquierdo, Bottom from left: Fred Littman, James Lee Hansen

businesses. There was no sense then that it would ever become the
glamorous neighborhood it is now.

Pain

At one point when I was in art school, I needed to go to the
dentist. The Oregon Health Sciences Dental School gave good care
at a very low cost. The visits were more time consuming because
everything involved a dentist teacher and a dental student. I hadn't
had a dental exam for a couple of years and my eating habits involved too much sugar. It turned out that every tooth in my head

needed work. This project extended over several months.

For philosophical reasons, I decided to experiment with having the drilling done without anesthetic. Mostly, I think, I wanted to see if I could put myself outside the pain. That is what I did. No anesthetic. The pain was intense, but when the drilling stopped, the pain stopped. I found I was sort of standing outside myself watching this happen. Eventually, I got all my teeth filled and fixed. (None had to be pulled.) There was one time, as I recall, that I couldn't divorce myself from the pain and that was when I had a bad hangover. I really felt it that morning. It was my own fault. Too much partying and drinking.

Manuel

At the beginning of my second year I met Manuel Izquierdo, a fellow student and we became very close friends. We were both living in the artist's colony on Upper Hall Street, a group of cottages built by a woman in the 1920s. Manuel and his brother Jose (Pepe) had a large cottage for which they paid $40 a month. Mine was a half size smaller and cost me $20. About a dozen wooden cottages perched on the hillside and nestled close together among the trees with wooden stairs going up to them and wooden walkways between. A fire in one of them would have wiped out all of them in minutes.

Manuel delivered the Oregonian in the mornings and he sometimes woke me for help when he slept in after a late night party. And we had a lot of parties in the cottages. He was able to afford a car, a nice old Model A Ford coupe that sat two in front and had a rumble seat that accommodated two more in the back. I

"Seventeen Bathers," oil, 1949.

had driven my folks' car, and had a license, so I taught Manuel to drive. We drove our girlfriends to the beach in that great little car. On the way, I remember passing mile after mile of the blackened snags of the great Tillamook Burn, the thousands of acres that had been consumed by a series of fires. The most recent fire had been only a couple of years before, in 1945.

Manuel was a quiet and reserved young man when I first knew him. He soon grew into the outgoing, frank, disarming, charming and outrageous person that was his true personality. He was a hard worker in school, as I was, and we both did a lot of art on our own, outside school assignments. During parties Manuel was always the catalyst for lots of hijinks. On evenings at Mike and Sally Russo's, he would sometimes disappear for a while and then make an entrance wearing one of Sally's dresses and carrying a mop on high, emulating the Statue of Liberty. He could mimic, with gusto and satiric effect, the Catholic liturgy. And he brought the same kind of realistic mimicry to flamenco singing and dancing.

A Duel

Around the art school and the museum, interesting escapades, seductions and rivalries abounded. Most everyone, it seemed, was young enough that libidos were always simmering, if that's the right word for what libidos do.

One of the rivalries that became general knowledge was between handsome European sculptor Fred Littman and World War II fighter pilot Museum Director Tom Colt over a lady who was Fred's girlfriend and model but who was also friendly with Tom Colt. It was said that Fred had challenged Colt to a duel over the matter. Some of this played out in a confrontation in the front row of the Guild Theater before the film started, with many of the art crowd in attendance. It was of course very entertaining. (The duel, however, didn't actually materialize). The Guild was the only movie house that played foreign films and therefore was the favorite of the artists.

Berlin Masterpieces

Some major shows came to the Art Museum, and one of them, in the early months after the end of the war, was "Masterpieces from the Berlin Museums." This was art that had been stored away in salt mines by the Germans during the war. At that time the art was in the possession of the US Army and was being exhibited in the US for a couple of years before being returned to the proper museums. The show had superb old master works including half a dozen Rembrandts. Since the works were in the custody of the Army, the collection was heavily guarded with soldiers in uniform with big side arms in their holsters. It was a wonderful show that I spent long hours absorbing.

"Decadent" Art

Another major show that came to the Art Museum while I was a student was a big exhibition of the works of three contemporary Spanish artists: Picasso, Miro and Gris. There were many works by each artist. This was a very exciting show, and one of the first of challenging modern art to come to Portland. It caused a great stir in the art community and people took sides about it. There were a couple of big, well attended panel discussions with titles like "Is Modern Art Decadent?" One of these was a panel of student participants of which I was one. I had a couple of weeks to prepare for it, and Louie and I had intense discussions over beer about the issue of "content" in art. By the morning of the panel I was well primed.

It took place in one of the galleries of the exhibition, and was attended by the whole student body and all the instructors, plus others, probably 125 people. It was set for 10 a.m. Bob Gallagher and Bennett Welch were two of the other student speakers. The anticipation was terribly nerve-wracking. Bob and I went across

Shirley, 1949

to the Broadway Inn (now Higgins) to calm our nerves. He had a beer. That would have upset my stomach so I just had coffee.

As is the case so often with talks, the nerve-wracking part is before you begin. Once you hear your own voice, you settle into a rhythm. It was exciting. Bennett took the side that modern art was decadent, I held the opposite, and we had a lively back and forth discussion with questions and statements from the audience. Afterward, everyone felt very energized.

Shirley

There was a nice payoff to my efforts. My talk made a strong impression on one very pretty, vivacious, and unconventional girl. Shirley Spackman was a joint Reed College-Museum Art School student. She was interested in dance as well as the visual arts and

Me above, Manuel, 1949

she asked me if I would like to go to a performance with her at Reed. I still had very limited experience with girls, and up to that point I felt that a date was a time when you had to somehow put on a performance. That was different with Shirley. Our conversations from the beginning were about things we were both interested in. With Shirley I felt I could be myself. We talked about art, dance, films and I didn't feel I had to try to be somebody else. She was my first real girlfriend. It was very intense and it lasted for about a year and a half and then she went away to Mills College. Later we did keep in touch from time to time over the years. She even showed up at my Governor's Award ceremony. She went on to do a doctorate specializing in dance history and to teach and publish original research on Baroque dance.

Some Student Successes

In 1950, I had a painting accepted in a national show of student art work and it was reproduced in Art News. I was one of 25 finalists for murals at the Washington State Capitol in Olympia. The possibility of actually doing a mural was dashed when the largest earthquake to hit the Northwest happened (1949). Subsequently they needed the funds to repair the cracked and damaged building, and the art projects were cancelled.

My first one-person show, in 1950, was at the Karouba Gallery, run at the time by Louie Bunce and his wife Eda. I was too self conscious to want to have an opening. It was a good show. It had no sales, but Louie and I traded paintings, and of course, that felt pretty special.

A Fresco Mural

During my last year at the Museum Art School, I was hired by Lucia Wiley (one of the instructors) to help her prepare the full scale drawings for the fresco that she was commissioned to do for the Tillamook County Courthouse that summer. She had a large house on the hillside overlooking Portland on SW Hall St. A long flight of stairs led up to the house. Her studio was a spacious room on the top floor with a wonderful view of the city. My job was to enlarge her smaller scale sketches to full size on paper that would

Working on the Tillamook fresco, Lucia Wiley, me,
1950

act as the guide for the painting. She had done several frescos before and was one of only a handful of artists in the United States
who had experience in that medium.

After the school year ended in June, Lucia and I went to Tillamook where I rented a room from a retired school teacher. For
the next three months worked as Lucia's assistant on the mural. I
would get up before dawn to begin to spray water into the plaster
wall to prepare it for the skilled plasterer, who arrived later to apply
the smooth coat of lime plaster. That was the area to be painted for
that day. I did a lot more which is too technical to go into here. At
one point, Lucia was dissatisfied with how the painting of a cow
had turned out. It was scraped off the wall and I was sent out to

make a drawing of another cow. Cows are everywhere around Tillamook. I made a drawing of one and that was used in the mural. I also drew and painted the cat and the grasshopper in the foreground. Overall I learned a lot from working on that mural with Lucia.

The mural is still in the lobby of the courthouse. The color is still luminous, though unfortunately, they have built a stairway that somewhat impedes the view of the mural's left hand side.

At the end of the summer, 1950, the mural finished, and with $400 savings in my pocket, I left for New York. The big city was 3,000 miles and several long days and nights away by Greyhound.

"The Building of the Morning Star," Lucia Wiley, fresco, 1950 Tillamook County Courthouse, Oregon

Printmaker Terry Haass, upper left, me in middle, Atelier 17, New York, 1950

Chapter Three

New York

I lived in New York from 1950 to 1953, arriving there as a 22-year-old art student fresh from the Museum Art School in Portland, Oregon. It was an interesting time to be in New York; the art community was still relatively small, and nobody was yet world famous.

Atelier 17

After my third year at the Museum Art School, I felt I had learned as much as I could there. In those days, 1950, the school did not offer a degree, only a certificate at the end of a four-year course. A certificate meant little in terms of teaching possibilities, so I saw no reason to stay on for a fourth year. New York was thought of by some artists as a kind of finishing school. The museums and galleries and the whole experience of being there could be a significant part of one's education. I had long planned to go there, and I thought I might enroll in a school, partly to have some contacts with artists. I had become very interested in printmaking as a result of my classes from Louie Bunce and Bill Givler at the Museum School, and the intaglio workshop Atelier 17 had a very good reputation. Stanley Hayter had been running it in New York through the war years, and though he had returned to Paris to re-establish his workshop there in 1949, his New York workshop was still going strong, being run then by some of his disciples.

I enrolled in the night classes at Atelier 17 at what was, even then, an extremely modest tuition, about $60 a year.

My first impression of the place was that it was physically pretty seedy. The premises had the appearance of what lots of older businesses in N.Y. still look like today; rickety, worn wooden stairs going up to the second floor. The Atelier itself consisted of a couple of good-sized rooms with two etching presses, an acid room and a small office space. Everything seemed to have ink on it, the wood floors, the presses and the margins of the proofs and the walls. This was an indication of the esthetics of William Hayter. He favored etchings with more plate tone, and he was never meticulous about wiping the edges of the plate, or keeping the paper margins clean.

But the atmosphere at Atelier 17 was very lively, with serious students and good professional artists who came there to make prints. Every once in a while a strait-laced sort of visitor would show up, casually look around, and since we weren't printing money on our presses, we didn't mind that they might come around to check on us now and then.

Karl Schrag

Atelier 17 offered beginning and advanced classes, each given twice a week in the evening. Since I hadn't done much etching, I enrolled in the beginning class. About 6 to 10 students attended each section. Karl Schrag was the instructor for both. He was a very good teacher and an excellent painter and printmaker, and he

Karl Schrag, "Self Portrait," oil, 1952

explained methods clearly. He was about 40, small boned and slen-
der with a balding head and beautiful dark eyes that glowed out of
a very compact head. You can look at any of his many self-portraits
to get a good sense of those eyes. He had a gentle sense of humor
that injected itself into his talks. "You put the aquatint rosin on
the plate and when you put the plate in the acid bath, the acid gets
very angry that it can't get at the whole plate so it furiously chews
little holes between the beads of rosin." Karl and I quickly became
good friends. And, without paying more tuition, I was soon permitted to attend both beginning and advanced classes. I was also
given a key to the place so that I could work on plates anytime.

   One day, Karl gave me a small Hayter etching proof that Hayter had left behind between some drying blotters. I still have it.

Ortman, Citron, Slivka

I met a number of artists, George Ortman, Minna Citron and David Slivka among them, who had worked at the Atelier and still came around to visit or to make prints. Ortman became a good friend. He was married, about my age, and a painter of geometric abstractions. He was a friend of artist Larry Rivers. I remember seeing a life-sized plaster figure sculpture of Rivers' sitting on the covered balcony porch of Ortman's apartment. Minna Citron was well off, and had a market for her work. She hired me to print some etchings for her at 50 cents a print. I was not an expert printer, but I managed. I worked from a proof of one of her prints and had to try to match it, which was difficult because very little of the image was actually in the plate. It was all surface tone. The poet Rithvan Todd used to come around, most of the time roaring drunk, but always full of funny stories. He had a wonderful, thick Irish accent. The sculptor David Slivka became a friend right off the bat, as did his then wife Rose, who later became editor of "Craft Horizon."

David loaned me his loft studio, which he was not using at the time, to live in for a couple of months before I found an apartment in a manufacturing district that was completely deserted at night. I had long, lonely blocks to walk to get there.

The loft was on the 4th floor of a garment manufacturing building which was empty at night. One bare light bulb illuminated each landing. The rest of the stairs were dark. I was happy to have the free rent, but it was a lonely place. I bought a recorder, the musical instrument, and used to practice late at night. From this

Don on our roof, Clinton Street, New York, 1952

distance in time, I can still hear that sound in the empty building. The bed was in the middle of the room under a big skylight, and it was a very pleasant place to wake up in in the morning, with the hum of the machinery on the floors beneath. There were a couple of other studios on that top floor, and during daytime hours I would see the other artists. One was Jose Guerrero, a very good abstract painter who had also done printmaking at Hayter's. In his work he used big squarish forms of different values floating against a ground. He was an advocate for abstract art and he used to say, "Find your own forms. Everyone has their own personal forms within."

Don Arrives

By February of 1951, my friend from junior high school days, photographer Don Normark, came to New York. When he arrived I met him at the bus depot, and by way of showing him the wonders of NY, I took him to an automat, a very large establishment where all the food was displayed on dishes in little cubicles behind glass doors. You would put coins in the slot and open the door to retrieve the sandwich or piece of pie. We were going along getting our selections, and the miracle of automation was working just fine, till Don tried unsuccessfully to get a cup of coffee with cream from a particular little window, trying over and over. Suddenly from behind a similar small window next to it and about waist high, a human head appeared and said, "What do you want, Bud? A cup of coffee with cream?" Don thought this was the funniest thing he had seen in a long time.

Cornelia Street

Don and I lived in a sub-lease in the West Village on Cornelia St (#22) which I had found through Terry Haass, who made prints and taught at Atelier 17. It was a little two-room apartment on the third floor, consisting of a main room about 15'x20,' with a tiny fake fireplace with a marble mantle, a small kitchen area with a table and a window-like opening between the kitchen and the other room. The bathtub was next to the sink and covered with a metal lid for washing the dishes when you weren't using the tub. The toilet was a tiny room, just big enough for the toilet, which we shared with the apartment next door. A door on either side had to be locked when you were in there and then unlocked when you finished, to make it available to the other apartment. The walls of the apartment were thin. A young married couple on the other side of one wall did a lot of loud verbal fighting and arguing. Then they made up and we were treated to the sounds of their ecstatic lovemaking.

A large Italian family lived in the apartment with which we shared the toilet. Somehow we never got to know them well. They shouted at us to shut up one night when we were sitting up late, drinking and talking. I think I had thrown an empty bottle at the fireplace to emphasize a point. The next day the wife knocked on our shared toilet door, and gave us a peace offering pie she had made.

We did get to know some of the other tenants. One was a good looking young woman with a year-old baby and no husband around. We invited her to dinner, soon after we first met her. Don and I were talking beforehand about how great it would be if we could get her to pose breastfeeding the baby, but thinking it would be too much to broach it to her. When she came to dinner she immediately sat down and began to nurse her baby with no inhibitions at all. We later had a couple of sessions making drawings and photos of her.

When we were first gathering furniture for the apartment we acquired a double bed. I think it fit the space better than two single beds. At any rate we got used to sleeping in the same bed even though one or the other of us would sometimes thrash around in our sleep. We had intended to get single beds, but never got around to it. Money was always at a premium, and nothing was ever purchased that was not a necessity. I'm sure some of our friends thought something funny was going on when they saw the one bed.

Don's Work

Don got a job with Look Magazine making prints in their dark-room. It paid about $1 an hour. He got to know some very well-known photographers and eventually assisted different ones on their assignments. Look Magazine was very powerful at that time, and was often visited by dignitaries of all sorts. He would come home from work and say, "Who do you suppose I saw in the corridors this morning?" The answer one time was "the Duke and Duchess of Windsor."

Sleeping In

Don and I tended to be very sound sleepers. This tendency was helped along by our keeping some very late hours. We were constantly sleeping through the alarm, and facing the consequences at work. We tried some ingenious methods to correct this. One way was to place the alarm clock on the sill of the open space between the kitchen and bed-living room. We carefully piled all the pots and pans on top of one another with the bottom pan perched on the turn key of the alarm clock. The next morning we woke an hour past alarm time. The pots and pans were strewn all over the floor. The end of this sleep syndrome came when I eventually went on a trip back to the West coast. Left to himself, Don abruptly found himself able to awake to the alarm clock, and I think that spelled the end of our hard-to-wake period.

Some luminaries were our neighbors. W.H. Auden lived a couple of doors north on Cornelia St. Auden, Don and I had the same dentist. "Circle in the Square" was an exciting off-broadway theater in the Village close by that was cheap and had excellent plays. I remember seeing Geraldine Page there before she got to be well known.

The Cedar Bar

Many of the active artists congregated at the Cedar Bar night after night. The Cedar was a working man's bar during the day, an artist's bar at night. It had almost nothing of what you would call atmosphere. A long narrow room, a bar on one side and high-backed booths down the other. The lighting was glaring and utilitarian. No pictures or decor on the walls. The lack of "atmosphere" and the rawness of the place suited the general attitude of the artists and the discussions that took place there.

The Cedar Bar was just down 8th St, about 6 or 8 blocks from Atelier 17. Our night sessions at the Atelier ended at 10 o'clock, and about twice a week a small group of us would walk over to the Cedar afterward. Most of the artists who later became famous were there regularly: DeKooning, Tworkov, Kline, Gottlieb, and many others. The conversations were very lively and the place was noisy, and of course full of smoke. All of us smoked in those days.

Critic Arthur Danto in "The State of the Art" said "The New York art world at the time was a scene of intensity and turbulence. Paintings of astonishing vitality and novelty were being produced by artists whose names are now legend, and who shouted themselves hoarse in a boozy protracted debate. It was a period of denunciation and controversy, of competing orthodoxies... in undertakings of near-religious urgency." And this is how it seems to me looking back.

Pollock

I remember seeing Jackson Pollock only once at the Cedar Bar. A group of about six of us had gone there after night classes: Karl Schrag, Terry Haass, Harry Hoehn and a couple of others. Half way down one side of the room, a round table was big enough to seat all of our group. The bar was crowded (it almost always was) and eventually, above the din came the sounds of loud angry, argument. It became apparent that it was Pollock in a drunken state. Almost everyone drank a lot in those days. But Pollock had a reputation for getting belligerent and picking fights when he was drunk. Someone in our group suggested that if he stopped at our table on his way out, we should not admit to being artists. "Let's make out that we are shoemakers from Chicago." We decided on the specialty each of us would supposedly be an expert in. Sure enough, as he passed our table, he stopped, lurching and weaving and, looking at the table, said, "It looks round, its round like Breugel." Then, sitting down, he spilled cigarettes from his package all over the table. When he asked us what we did, we began our charade. That worked for a while as we described our shoemaking craft, and the specialties we each supposedly did. But he eventually got suspicious and left in a huff. It wasn't very nice of us, but it seemed funny at the time.

The Gallery Scene

In 1950, the social life of New York artists took place within a small number of blocks, between about 4th and 6th Avenues and 8th to 10th Streets. In addition to the Cedar Bar and Atelier 17, the Hans Hoffman School, consisting of Hans Hoffman, teacher, the Artists Club, and some cooperative galleries, such as the Tanager. The uptown galleries had for many years focused on European art and by 1950 still had very little interest in American artists. The scene would change in the next few years, but at that time the artists were still forced to fend for themselves, having shows where they could. Of course, very few made sales. One very important exhibition that took place in 1951 was a big group show of all the artists who later became important. The artists got together and rented a large storefront space on 9th St and had a 20-day show consisting of about 60 artists' works. This show caused a lot of interest within the artists' community. It was all new abstract expressionist work.

The Artists Club

The Artists Club was another cooperative venture. It was an inadequately heated place on a second floor, where people kept their overcoats on in the winter. Like many old NY interiors, it had wooden floors and molded tin ceilings. Thirty-five cents covered the cost of admission and drinks from gallon jugs of cheap red wine. Meetings were held every Friday night with a speaker or a panel discussion on a given topic. Some of the panel topics were: "What We Don't Have To Do Anymore," "What's Wrong With Wrong?" and "Who Owns Space?" A lot of discussion centered around the issue of *space* in painting and in sculpture. My friend David Slivka organized a panel of sculptors: Lassaw, Noguchi, David Smith and himself. The topics of individual speakers were extremely varied, and covered music, too. John Cage, Merce Cunningham, and Morton Feldman were some of the people I heard there.

While the Club was organized by visual artists, the topics ranged all over the place and included science, philosophy, even religion. Anything was game for discussion. What a time that was! The artists were hungry for debate and discussion, and they thrived on it.

I was fascinated by all the talk and by the intensity of it. At the same time, I found much of it far too full of generalities for what I wanted at the time.

New York School

By 1950, World War II had been over for five years. Many of the European artists who had lived in New York during the war, and had infused the art scene with vital ideas and attitudes, had gone back to Europe. There were lots of new art students as a result of the GI bill. The artists were full of optimism, and they knew and believed by that time that there was a way out from under the powerful influence of Europe and Picasso. Picasso had been the dominating force in art for 40 years or more. He had invented everything and had moved into every possible area of art. He had become, in a sense, a huge albatross around the necks of the artists. But by 1950, the New York artists had begun moving aggressively into areas that were very unPicasso-like, areas of art that Picasso had not delved into. Among these were: enormous size, complete abstraction, paint itself as the subject of painting, and the issue of flatness as the essence of the work. These were the qualities that gave the American artists room to operate.

"New Yorkscape-'51," oil, painted in 1980 as a memory of New York.
Middle left: me, Mrs. Fenway and her dog, Van Gogh on his way to paint.
Lower left: de Kooning, painter Jack Tworkov, Don.

Prices

The magazine Art News used to quote price ranges when reviewing gallery shows. Some of the prices from 1950 and 1951: Ad Reinhard $150-250, Hans Hoffman $500-1300, Mark Rothko $500-1500, Larry Rivers $50-1000, Helen Frankenthaler $50-800, Lee Krasner $350-1500, Adolph Gottlieb $500-1500, Joan Mitchell $100-800, Pollock $250-3000 (one of the highest).

In price, prints lagged far behind for many years. Atelier 17 used to have annual shows of the group of artist printmakers who worked there. One show included prints by Miro, Tanguy, Corbusier, Mason and Schrag at $5-150. The following year, 1951, lists a show of original Picasso prints at $75-150!

Parties

There were a lot of parties, mostly at various artists' studios. Because of the small size of the art community at the time, and because nobody was that famous, the parties were very accessible. You found out about one by word of mouth and just showed up. Everyone smoked Pall Malls. They were, I think, the only long cigarette. With those, you got more for your money. Cheap red wine by the gallon jug was the standard party drink. The Tarantella seemed to be the unofficial official dance at the artists' parties at the time. Everyone drank to excess at all the parties. But it was all friendly. I remember sitting next to DeKooning, listening to him talk. He spoke with a heavy Dutch accent, was interested in everything under the sun, and was a really nice guy. John Cage and Merce Cunningham were among the party regulars. Parties went on until the small hours and you often went to a Rikers all night cafeteria afterwards. Very cheap simple food. A sausage on a bun and coffee.

DeKooning

I first saw DeKooning's paintings of women at the Stable Gallery, which had been a horse stable not many years before, during the days when deliveries were made with horses. I think there was still a ramp leading from the first floor to the second, where they had led the horses up to the stalls. The DeKooning women paintings were first shown in 1951. That show was only about the third one he'd had, though he had been painting for many years. These paintings caused a great stir, and I responded to them strongly. Coming from the Museum Art School, I had cut my teeth on German Expressionism, and I saw a strong relationship between that movement and the de Koonings. But some artists criticized him for "backsliding." Introducing the figure back into painting was felt to be a betrayal of the abstract expressionist credo. In the end, of course, everyone had to put up with what he had done because it was such powerful painting, and it did, after all, involve an emphasis on paint and ambiguous spatial structure that fit the new "look."

Incidentally, there was lots of talk about painting having a "look." Probably this was because Abstract Expressionism never was one particular style. So referring to a "look" was a convenient way of summarizing the qualities that were beginning to be felt as the "New York School." Nevertheless, the word "look" annoyed me because it sounded so much like a fashion term.

Clinton Street

Don and I had lived in the Cornelia St. sublet apartment for a few months when the principal renter wanted the place back. So we had to move. After searching for some time, we found a cold water flat on Clinton Street in the lower East side. Clinton is an extension of Avenue C between Houston (pronounced Howston) and Delancey Streets. There were two apartments of two rooms each, and one water spigot, of cold water only, in each unit. No furniture except a fridge and a gas two-burner hot plate. The other unit, down the hall, had been used to house monkeys and retained a strong odor of monkey urine. These two rooms became my studio and Don's darkroom. The shared toilet was at the end of the hall. No bathtub. We would sponge-bathe, or take baths at friends' places. Whenever I went to dinner at Karl Schrag's he would say, "Would you like to take a bath before dinner?" I was probably more pleasant to have around after I bathed.

Jewish District

The apartment on Clinton St was about six blocks from the nearest subway stop. You would walk along Houston St past small grocery stores, past famous Katz's Delicatessen, step over half a dozen drunks sprawled unconscious on the sidewalk, turn the corner on Clinton and half way down the block opposite the Palestine Theater was our doorway, number 26. At that time the neighborhood was predominately Jewish, with many kosher shops. A bakery sold a great heavy dark rye bread. We were two blonde young men and the woman proprietor would say "What do you want, goyim boys?" The Mogen David Wine Company was also in the neighborhood and we bought it by the gallon jug. It was terribly sweet, but it was cheap. We also bought a very good cheesecake by the slice at the corner grocery.

Summer Nights

Don's and my apartment was on the second floor. The buildings in that neighborhood were about 5 stories tall. In the summer with the windows open, the street sounds and voices made it seem everyone was in one big living room. And of course, in New York, the street life goes on till 3 or 4 in the morning. One night when Manuel Izquierdo was visiting, staying with us for a couple of weeks, a very drunk guy was singing and swearing on the street below at about 2 a.m. He was across the street, and people in the building above him kept shouting down at him to SHUT UP! Finally, someone in the window directly above him pored a full bucket of water down on him. This stopped him for a while and he moved farther down the street under the marquee of the Palestine Theater. The three of us decided to be good Samaritans and we went down to take him a towel and a dry shirt. He turned out to be an ex-prize fighter and kind of belligerent, but at least we did our good deed.

At another time, for several months, across the street a fellow of about 70, with asthma, used to lean out his window at night and cough and cough. He was heavy set and his cough was like the roar of a lion. Of course, this kept others from sleeping and there were constant shouts from the neighbors of FOR GOD'S SAKE SHUT UP AND LET US GET SOME SLEEP. Finally, he had a fatal seizure amid great commotion and shouts from the two women who lived with him. A crowd filled the street looking up at the window on the third floor across from me. "A man! A man!" they shouted. No one was doing anything, so I rushed downstairs and up to their apartment. He was lying on the floor and it was apparent he was already dead. I helped lift him back onto the bed and tried to reassure the ladies that he would be OK. Then an ambulance came and took away. The nights were somewhat quieter after that.

Summer Windows

Many of the women in the Lower East Side used the window like the TV is used now. They would put a pillow on the sill, and sit on a chair in front of the window, leaning on their elbows, watching the street activity for hours.

The summers were so hot and humid as to be almost unbearable. One summer activity on the lower East side was to open a fire hydrant. There was a great blast of water the kids ran in and out of. This was, of course, illegal. But the cops didn't always shut it off right away. I once saw a cop standing around a corner from an open hydrant, peering at it, just watching, and enjoying it.

Studio Heating

We installed a gas burning stove for heat in the front apartment, and we had a double gas burner for cooking. For heat, my studio in the back apartment had only a potbelly coal stove. We were on the second floor, a walk-up, of course, and I had to carry sacks of coal up to the studio. The trouble was I could never get a good fire going, and in the winter, I was reduced to wearing my Salvation Army overcoat and gloves in order to paint. It is very cumbersome trying to mix oil paint wearing thick woolen gloves. One day the stove was going out, and I picked up a small container of turpentine, opened the stove door, and threw it in to encourage the fire. There was a muffled "kaboom" and heavy black smoke began, in slow motion, to loom out of the stove and upward. I was able to dash around the room, and pick up all the paintings, hustle them into the adjoining room, and close the door before the cloud hit the ceiling and began to descend, covering everything with soot.

Finding Street Furniture

We bought furniture from the Goodwill and also made some from wooden crates that we found in the streets. Once we found a nice sofa abandoned on the street, and we hauled it several blocks back to the apartment. What a prize! It probably took only about an hour before we were hustling it and its infestation of fleas down the stairs, and back to the street. The apartment already had its own problem with vermin. Besides cockroaches, bedbugs hid in the irregular cracks of the plaster walls and came out at night as soon as the lights were turned out. We were constantly pumping some kind of bug spray into the cracks. My God, how did we ever entice girlfriends to a place like that? Somehow we did.

Mrs. Fenway

Our apartment had a bright red door; I don't remember if we painted it or if it was already that color. We never locked it. One woman in her 60s, a Mrs. Fenway, lived alone in an apartment on the ground floor with her German Shepherd. She befriended us, and she was in the habit of coming right in without knocking, any time day or night. We had to ask her finally to please knock

Me, Bayard Rustin, 1951

before entering, and she was sort of offended. Her German Shepherd slept on a folding cot next to her bed. They were constant
companions, and she talked to it in the same way one would talk
to a person. The dog seemed to understand everything she said.
One evening we met her returning from a walk just outside the
apartment building. The dog had wanted some stick it had seen a
block or so back down the street. We were talking about it and she
said to him, "Oh, all right you can have it" in a perfectly conver-
sational voice, and he immediately lit out down the street to get it.
Mrs. Fenway liked to drink whiskey, and she would give the dog
a saucer full, which he'd lap up and get very drunk, going round
and round, as if he had a hard time finding the floor to lie down.

There were a lot of other young people living in our building.

One was Rick Basoyan, who was writing a musical play, which became "Little Mary Sunshine." It eventually became a great success and is still performed all around the US. This was the only play of his that was successful. He later committed suicide, but I don't know if this was related to his career, or what.

Bayard Rustin

Bayard Rustin, the great civil rights activist, became a friend and came to dinner a couple of times at our apartment. We had a great recipe for lentil soup, with sausage and spices and was very thick. It was the constant specialty of our house when we had guests. Bayard was a tall, handsome black man who had studied at Oxford. He had a beautiful speaking voice with a cultivated English accent, which, with his dignified bearing, gave him an imposing presence. I suppose he worked to acquire that accent, but it seemed absolutely convincing. Don and I attended a couple of civil rights seminars and went on marches with him and his group of activists. One, I remember, was in Philadelphia. I recall being with a large group of people sleeping overnight on the floor in someone's very large apartment. Bayard was one of those heroically brave people who were working for desegregation in the deep South in the late 40s and early 50s, long before civil rights gained the national spotlight, when it was very easy to get killed doing that kind of work. Ten years after we knew him, he was the principal organizer for Martin Luther King's March on Washington.

Central Park Mugging

Sometime during the winter of '51, Don was entertaining a girlfriend, and he wanted to have the apartment to themselves for the evening. I went out, and it was expected that I would not return till about midnight. I went to a movie, and then around 11 p.m. I found myself on 5th Avenue, next to Central Park around 75th St. For some reason I decided to go for a walk in the park. In those days it wasn't tantamount to suicide to walk in Central Park at night by oneself, but it was still not a judicious thing to do. About a block into the park, there is a large circular bowl, with broad steps going down to a central stage space. Lamp posts surround it, and it is fairly well lit. At first, no one else was around. I was about half way down the steps when I noticed a figure walking along the other side of the bowl, near the top. Then another figure appeared on the other side, and began to casually descend down toward where I was headed. I suddenly did not want to be there. They were between 5th Avenue and me. The only place to go was farther on into the dark trees. I suddenly took off running up the side and away from these two guys. They took off after me. I was a good runner, but it was pitch black and after a couple of hundred yards of running with low branches clawing at my face, my glasses were knocked off. I stopped and listened. No one was following. I needed those glasses. I started crawling along on hands and knees, feeling the leafy ground, searching for them. Somehow I found them. I scrambled out of the park and got to 5th Avenue as fast as I could. I must have been a great sight when I got back to the apartment. "What the hell happened to you?" asked Don, who for his part, had had a lovely evening.

Pacifism

Being a pacifist was a big factor in my life. Jack McLarty's anti-war sentiments and my discussions with him had influenced me very strongly. In 1947, when I was granted conscientious objector status, there was no war on. The Korean war started in the summer of 1950, and by the time I got to New York, a young man's draft status was a big deal, especially to potential employers, who wanted to know how long you were going to be around. There were very few COs in those days. The mass objection to war that came later, during Vietnam, would have seemed very far-fetched back then. So it was lonely to be in that position. I was sure of the rightness of my conviction, and there was nothing to do but maintain it. But I was made to feel like a pariah when I applied for work, and the potential employer learned I was a CO. I really felt like an outsider. Of course, among artists it was a different matter. Most of them already felt they were true outsiders.

The Quakers

I eventually became acquainted with the Quakers, and I met people at the Fellowship of Reconciliation, a long-time pacifist organization. There I met A.J. Muste, a famous, old, long time pacifist. He was a very kindly, gaunt, gray-haired gentleman, who had lots of good counsel later when I had to face hearings before the draft board in N.Y. David Dellinger was another pacifist I met who had spent time in prison during W.W.II and who wrote a book "From Yale to Jail," which is well worth reading. I began attending Quaker meetings in Brooklyn, at a meeting house where the attendance on Sundays was a couple of hundred. The benches were arranged in a tiered, rectangular, box-like area. And it was quite a mystical experience to sit in silence with 200 other people. You were only supposed to get up to speak if called upon by the holy spirit. Otherwise, it was an intense silence for the hour. The Quaker meetings were a very rich experience.

I began going to a Quaker center in Manhattan to help bundle clothing that was being sent for European relief. A small group of us, Quakers and others, met a couple of times a week to volunteer for this task.

Losing My Draft Card

One night sometime in my second year in New York, I was headed downtown on the subway late at night, when I fell asleep. I woke up, and looked out the train window to find the station numbers increasing, instead of decreasing, and realized I had gone all the way to the end of the line, and was on my way back uptown. I also realized that my wallet was gone.

One of the cards I had to replace was my draft card. The law required every man of draft age to carry one. So, without thinking too much about it, I sent a letter to my draft board in Seattle, asking for a new card to replace the old one. I was surprised to receive a letter back, with a new card, informing me I was now classified IA and to report to the draft board in N.Y. What a shock!

Thus began an odyssey of a year and a half of hearings and preparing for hearings, before the draft board. There were actually only two hearings, but a lot of time was spent talking to friends in preparation at the Quakers and Fellowship of Reconciliation.

Draft Board Hearing

The first hearing was before a New York draft board, six or eight men. They were not sympathetic listeners. At one point, as I was going into a long answer to a question, one of them interrupted me said: "Who's been feeding you this line of crap?" I tried to talk about my conviction that pacifism was more than just a stance concerning the army, that it was a philosophy of life, and a way of living. And of course, I brought up my volunteer work with the Quakers, and of my attendance at Quaker services. In the end, they said they were going to recommend I be given a noncombatant's army classification. I said I would not accept that, because that would still be aiding the military and was against my conscience.

My hearing was the last item of the evening for the board, and they adjourned. I rode down in the elevator with a couple of the board members. We talked a bit and I said: "Well, I'll go to prison rather than accept that classification." One of the men said "No, I don't think you will. You're not that type. You'll take it." "No I won't," I responded. It was sort of a surreal exchange, now that I think about it.

After receiving the new classification in the mail, I wrote back saying I would not accept it. Then I was given a new hearing date before an appeal judge.

The hearing date was a couple of months away. And I did a lot of thinking and worrying about the real possibility of going to prison for two years. But I never considered giving in. I kept an intermittent diary during the New York years, which I recently read through. One entry close to the hearing date states, "I am completely tranquil and resigned to the possibility of going to prison." From this vantage point, so many years later, it is hard to imagine how I was able to arrive at that tranquility.

Second Hearing

Five or six different judges heard draft appeals. Some were known to be "hanging judges," very unsympathetic. Somehow I lucked out and drew one with a better reputation for fairness. I rehearsed questions and answers with pacifist friends who knew the ropes. Before the hearing, I got letters of character reference from a number of my friends. Don Normark and an older friend, Hobart Mitchell, a Quaker, went along with me. There was one big table in a smallish room, with the three of us and the judge seated at it. He began by asking straightforward questions, and I remember that in spite of all the rehearsals, I began stumbling over my words, and I was not very smooth at all. But at one point, the judge asked about the hearing that took place when my status was changed from 4E to 1A. "There was no hearing," I said. "They just sent me a new classification." His whole demeanor changed. "We don't need to go any farther with this hearing," he said. I offered him the half dozen character letters I had brought along. "I won't need those." he said. He didn't say what he would do but just said the meeting was over.

I realized then, that the Seattle board's breach of procedure had given me a chance for freedom. It was a week or two before I heard from the board, but I was pretty certain what the outcome would be. The new classification came and it was 4E, conscientious objector status. I would be required to do alternative service

"MacArthur Parade Watchers", Don Normark, 1951

with some approved charitable organization. So that was it. What a relief! Now it was up to me to find a suitable group to let me spend two years with them. That was a chore in itself. But after thinking about working in a mental hospital and approaching the Lutherans, who didn't want me since I was not a practicing Lutheran, and thinking about maybe going with the Mennonites, I decided on the Quaker's Mexico work camps and was accepted.

Incidentally, being a CO must have been a big deal, and a threat, to the authorities in those days, because before my hearings, as I found out later the FBI spent countless man-hours interviewing friends, relatives, and employers.

Work

When I first arrived in New York in the fall of 1950, I had

$400 that I had saved up over a period of time. After several weeks I found a job, before my money ran out. It would have been embarrassing to have to return to Portland if I couldn't find work. The first job I got was through Minna Citron, who had studied at Hayter's workshop and was well to do and had lots of connections. Through her I found work in a large office of a construction firm that built skyscrapers. They employed lots of engineers and architects. My job was to itemize beams and columns in pages which listed hundreds of I beams, T beams, and various kinds of columns, and to check one list of these items against another list. A job, in short, that I was eminently unsuited for. I was a dreamy expressionist painter, and there was no way I could keep my concentration on this kind of exacting minutia. It hurts one's ego to be fired from a job, and I certainly needed the work, but that kind of task is just not my cup of tea. I lasted about a month.

Frame Shop

Then I began pounding the pavement, looking for work, going from one store to another to see if they needed help. Eventually, I inquired at a frame shop, Falcor Frames. It was run by an Italian fellow named Falcone, who was in his mid-50s. I went to work for him making frames and tending to customers. $1 an hour, no benefits. He had one other employee, a teenage high school student who worked part-time. It was an ordinary, run-of-the-mill frame shop that made inexpensive frames in standard sizes. My main job was to sit at a treadle machine, which chopped the molding at a 45-degree angle. It was all leg power and it took energy to do that for hours on end. Falcone was a gruff sort of guy but okay to work for. He was a conservative Republican, but he knew what my ideas were, and he tolerated them, even my pacifism. I was working there at the time of the MacArthur parade. Douglas MacArthur had been fired by Truman and was returning to America to a huge New York ticker tape parade. Falcone was very pro-MacArthur. He closed the shop for the day, and gave me the day off, without pay. I didn't go to the parade. But Don went and made a set of wonderful, biting photographs of the adoring MacArthur crowds.

Baseball

Falcone was a great baseball fan, particularly a fan of the NY Giants. The Giants were playing the Brooklyn Dodgers in the last game of the regular season in 1951. I went on an errand for the shop, and, walking along the street block after block, I could follow the game, because everyone, everywhere, had the radio tuned to the game. The Giants had been trailing the Dodgers all season, but they were even with them in the standings by the last game. In the bottom of the 9th they were behind by three runs with two out. At that point, the Giant batter hit a home run with the bases loaded, which won the game and the league championship for the Giants. Falcone was leaping all over the place with joy, as was much of the city.

Slaughter House

Eventually, I asked Falcone for a raise, without success. So I started to look for other work. Don and I heard that they were hiring at a slaughter house on the West side by the Hudson River, and

"Slaughter House," oil, 1951

we both applied. It was one of only a couple of slaughter houses on Manhattan. It was kosher, and the meat had to be on the dinner table within three days of being butchered. The hiring officer was a real right-wing type with a pseudo-military mentality. For some reason he did not inquire about my draft status. Otherwise, I'm sure I would not have been hired.

We were hired along with quite a few others. And the money was pretty good. It was a huge building. They killed chickens, lambs and steer. Don and I worked in separate parts of the plant. I was in the cold locker, where the calf carcasses were hung up by the hind legs after slaughter. With the hide partly skinned off, it hung down onto the floor like a beautiful royal robe. My job was to grab hold of the hide, swing the carcass away, and at the same time, pull down so that the hide was torn the rest of the way off. This work was very heavy and exhausting. By mid-day, I didn't think I had the strength to finish out the day. But somehow, the necessity of keeping the job prevailed over tired muscles. And after several days of this kind of work, I got stronger.

It was the hottest part of summer, August. New York was stiflingly hot. However, after working in the cold locker for eight hours, my temperature was lowered to the point where I was perfectly comfortable for three or four hours in the 95 degree outside heat.

One bonus of that job was this: it provided fascinating subject matter. I started going up to the slaughter floor during my lunch hour, and making drawings. The slaughter area was a huge space, not refrigerated, that reminded me of Francis Bacon's paintings. This is where they killed the steers. Chains were wrapped around the ankles of the hind legs, and the huge beasts would be hoisted up out of the stall by an overhead crane. Since they weighed close to a ton I'm sure it was very painful and they bawled from pain and fright. The killing was done by rabbis, or at least by butchers with rabbi's training. They were men with long beards, who wore heavy dark leather aprons and were often shirtless because of the heat. They carried a 30-inch long sword about three inches wide. This was kept sharp with frequent honing. A helper would grab the hanging steer's nostrils with a pair of tongs, and pull the head toward himself, stretching the neck out. At this point, the butcher would put the sword to the neck and pull upward with a deft stroke. The bawling stopped like a radio suddenly turned off, the steer's eyes rolled upward and a river of blood gushed down to the floor and washed toward the floor drain. The kicking and quivering continued for a time, but meanwhile, the steer would be pushed along by an overhead trolly out of the way to make room for the next victim. The stench of blood was awful, and that, of course, also frightened the cattle that were on their way in, or waiting their turn in the stalls.

Slaughter Drawings

All of this was fascinating to watch, and I have to say that although I felt for the animals in an intellectual way, I did not respond with the same gut feelings that I would today. I needed to get permission from the management to make drawings. This was at a time long before the animal liberation movement got started, but there was still apprehension on the part of the slaughterhouse, that any visual renditions of what went on there, could be used in ways that would put them in a bad light. I was able to convince the management that I was a fine artist and only wanted subject matter for my personal painting. So I was able to do a lot of sketches, and I did a number of paintings from them.

Getting Fired

After about two weeks, the foreman of my department came

to me and said, "I'm going to have to let you go. I'm sorry, because you are a good worker, but I have orders from the office." So I was fired without a reason and didn't find out why until a few days later, when Don was fired. It seems the hiring person, Lenny, a Nazi type, had looked at Don's resume, and found that he had attended the New School For Social Research (he took writing classes under the GI Bill). The New School had a reputation for being very left wing, even Communist. This was too much for the fascist, and Don had to be let go, and along with him, his friend George. Incidentally, this incident surfaced later in the draft hearing before the judge: "Were you ever fired from a job for being a Communist?" The FBI had done a diligent job of digging up worthless innuendo.

Heidenryck

I went back to work for Falcone for a while, still at $1 an hour. But then I was introduced to the House of Heidenryck, probably through some artist acquaintance. The House of Heidenryck was one of the most prestigious frame shops in New York. They did custom frames for places like the Museum of Modern Art, and for many big collectors. Henry Heidenryck was a man of about 55 then, a very gentle, self-effacing sort of person, who spoke somewhat hesitantly. He was a very kind person. I learned somehow, not through him, that his family back in Holland had risked their lives to hide and help many Jews during the Nazi occupation. I told him I had been making $1.00 an hour at my former framing job and he said, "My, that's not very much, is it?" I started at about $1.50, and he wanted me to work on the sales floor. Heidenryck would design frames for specific paintings. I remember one in particular, a simple but heavy, rounded, blonde wood frame with a gold insert that he named the Siloti, designed by Mr. Hydenryck especially for a big brassy Picasso, owned by the Museum of Modern Art. Many other shapes were designed for specific paintings. That new design would then become part of the stock of frames that could be used for other paintings.

Office Work

Working in the office as a salesman meant that I had to wear a sports coat and tie. Considering the clientele they had, the House of Hydenryck had a rather modest office and showroom. One other young man, also a painter, sat at one desk, and I sat at the other, ready to wait on customers. There were racks of frames and samples, all crowded into a couple of not very large rooms. And there was no air conditioning! The place became absolutely stifling in the summer, and I would pour sweat into my nice white shirt. I don't know how the clients stood it.

When a painting, often by a top-notch painter (Rouault, Braque, Chagall) was brought in for framing, my job was to help choose the frame and finish that would most enhance the particular work of art. I did all this on the basis of no special training except for my art school background. I'm not sure I was always right, but I think my choices were pretty good on the whole. The downside of the job was that when no clients were around, I had to sit at the desk and appear busy, when there was really nothing to do. I hated this.

Heidenryck liked to hire working artists. I'm sure he knew that he was getting a bonus, because of the taste we brought to

Heidenryck frame shop workers from right: me, Chris, Henry Heidenryck in suit, 1952

the job. The frame fitting room was across the hall from the sales room. Seong Moy, a very good abstract woodcut artist who already had a reputation, worked in the fitting room doing various jobs, including some art restoration when needed.

The frames were very expensive. Many were hand carved, some were gold leafed, many were custom-made for the particular art work. Sometimes an artist would come in to have something framed, without realizing the expensive nature of the place. I remember showing a frame to such an artist and feeling embarrassed for him when he was aghast at the price I quoted him. I, of course, couldn't afford such prices any more than that artist could.

"The Framemaker" (Chris) 1952
Collection: Joan Darling and William Jones

Moving to the Frame Shop

After a couple of months in the office, I asked Henry if I could transfer to the frame making shop, which was located in a two story building a couple of blocks away. I had had enough of office life and knew I would be happier working with my hands. Henry approved, as he did with most requests. I had earlier asked for a raise, with positive results. Thus began a really enjoyable time for me as a frame finisher.

The Workers

The shop employed about a dozen people including three or four wood carvers, who were Italian immigrants who spoke limited English. Hugo, a good looking Italian of about 30, was shop foreman, and an older fellow, a Norwegian who had been a painter, was in general charge. He no longer did any painting, but he had a handsome little 12"x16" still life painting of his hanging in his office. He had known one of the respected New England artists who had said he admired that painting. He was holding on to that statement as something that warmed him, and validated his past as a painter. Early on, he questioned me about my commitment to art, as if it was something improper, and said, "You should get married, settle down and earn a living and don't spend so much time painting. You are neglecting your duty to society."

There were several other frame finishers besides me, (some were, or had been, artists). Another was a black guy named Chris, who applied plaster molds, imitation carving, to wood frames. Chris had been in the army (though I think not in combat), and became quite disturbed when I told him I was a conscientious objector. Several of the others joined in the discussion, and I remember Hugo saying to Chris, "Why don't you ease off? This is a question of his religion. Don't bother him about it." We eventually became quite friendly, which was good, because we worked in the same area of the shop. But he liked to try to get under my skin. The radio would be on, and when news came on about American troops engaging hordes of Chinese in Korea, he would say as a way of needling me, "That's rugged, man, those guys are rug-ged!"

Milo and Steve

Milo Pierre Antoine, one of the other frame finishers, was a tall, slim Haitian, who on learning that I was a CO said, "You ought to be in prison." It turned out later that he meant it ironically, and he had never heard of such a thing as a CO before. He and I became good friends, and would go together to the local diner for lunch. When we had known each other for a couple of weeks, he hinted that he was gay. Then he asked whether by chance, I might be inclined that way. When I said I was not, that was that, and we went on being friends. Steve (I don't recall his last name) was another frame finisher, and also gay. He was tall and blonde and looked something like movie actor Van Johnson. He had been an artist sometime in the past, but no longer painted. The three of us became quite close. Steve was a gourmet cook and we would have elaborate meals at his apartment. And since Don had left for Italy by then, they became my closest friends for quite a while.

The Joy of the Work

Heidenryk did a lot of antique finishing on frames, and many of the frames I worked on were "pickled" finishes. Pickling amounted to taking a raw wood, usually oak, frame and raking it down its length with a serrated tool that would claw out the softer parts of the grain. Then a gesso would be applied, various "dusts," (powdered pigments), would be brushed into the grooves, and a shoe polish of brown or black would be rubbed on the high spots with a rag. All of this gave a very convincing effect of weather-worn old wood of considerable age. The color effect was controlled so that it complimented the particular painting it was made for. We would imitate wormholes in the wood with a small drill. At times a frame beautifully carved with roses, would be required to look aged. I would take up my claw tool, and go to work on it, knocking off chunks of the carving before beginning the pickling job. How the old carvers winced at that. Though they knew the antiquing was part of the process, it must have hurt to see their beautiful work brutalized. I also made mat inserts for the frames by gluing various cloths to beveled masonite.

In fact, I had a great deal of satisfaction in the job. I was able to follow through with a frame from start to finish. And I would wake up in the morning and think, "Oh boy, I get to go to work, and finish that frame I started yesterday." I was so involved with the frames we made that I would go to an exhibition at the Modern, say, and catch myself looking first at the frames, before I looked at the pictures. How embarrassing!

One other plus of the job, was that, because of Heidenryk's sympathy for artists, we could take a day off, almost whenever we wanted it. Without pay, of course. But I did often call in to say I was staying home to paint.

Living Cheap

I was painting every day. On days when the frame shop took

eight hours of my time, I painted after work till two or three in the morning. Eventually, I arranged to be put on part-time, working a four-hour day so that I could have more time in the studio. This, of course, cut my salary in half (to about $25 a week), but time was more valuable than the extra money, and my needs were simple. Clothes were almost entirely from the Goodwill. I don't think I ever had a pair of shoes that really fit. I presumed that they were going to pinch in some way or other, and I just had to live with it. I had a heavy woolen overcoat that cost 50 cents and was warm, though it weighed about 20 pounds. I found that I could make a bottle of whiskey last a long time by taking a shot glass to the studio, and sipping the tiniest of sips from it for the whole evening. I smoked a couple of packs of cigarettes a day, but they were about 20 cents a pack. The subway was 5 cents. So was the Staten Island Ferry. Going across to the Island was a nice, long trip for a nickel. And there were a lot of free things to do, such as lectures at Cooper Union school.

I had no telephone. I would get a telegram from a girlfriend when I was painting away in my studio, saying, "Come over." (Telegrams were delivered by hand, a couple of hours after sending. I read recently that Edward Albee had supported himself by delivering telegrams in that part of Manhattan at about that time. If he delivered one to me, the tip would have been pretty meager.)

Settlement House Teaching

My first job of teaching art was at a Settlement House (a Community Center) on the upper East side. There were sports activities upstairs and classes in various subjects in the basement. I taught two nights a week from seven to ten. "Taught" is kind of a euphemism, since it was more like being a warden trying to keep some kind of order. The main idea was to keep the kids off the street for as long as possible. The children I taught were from age seven to about 13 and they could come and go as they pleased, so it was a big accomplishment to actually interest them in a project.

Teaching there was a great experience, and I took it seriously. I kept introducing different projects and there was a lot of satisfaction when I could manage to get the kids interested. There were some wonderfully sweet kids. One little 8-year-old Hispanic boy with curly hair used to enter the room running, fall to his knees, and skid forward with his arms raised over his head. What an entrance! Some of them did very aggressive pictures, which had a lot to do with their dysfunctional home lives and the tough street life. I was continually trying to get them away from doing war scenes (the Korean war was on). One of the boys would say, "You won't put my work up if I do a war scene, will you?" But they got to know that I cared about them, and there were some real satisfactions to the job. It lasted for the length of the term, four or five months.

Art Exhibitions, Visitors

Rembrandt's "Aristotle Contemplating the Bust of Homer" was purchased by the Metropolitan Museum in about 1952 for just over $1,000,000, the highest price ever paid for any work of art. Long lines of New Yorkers waited to view it. I visited the Met during that time, and one could go to the other parts of the Museum without waiting in line. The gallery where other superb

Rembrandts were on display was empty of visitors. Money is what the crowds were there to see.

The Kraushaar Gallery, where Karl Schrag and other good artists showed their work, had a show of paintings from Oregon which included Mike Russo, Carl Morris, Tom Hardy, among others. As a result of this show, the latter two were picked up by the gallery and showed there for many years.

Portland's Louie Bunce was given a show in the New Talent Gallery of the Museum of Modern Art in 1951. This was in a gallery on the top floor, which was associated with the member's lunchroom. It was a modest venue, but it was part of the Museum of Modern Art. Louie didn't come to NY for the show, however, because of his teaching schedule.

Whenever visitors came to town, we would go around to see everything interesting. Jack McLarty came and stayed for ten days, sleeping on the studio floor. On one occasion, late in the afternoon, we decided to go to the Frick Collection to see their great Rembrandt self-portrait. It was a long trip uptown and after walking to the subway, taking the train and changing trains, we arrived with 15 minutes to spare before closing. We went straight to the Rembrandt, drank it in, and that was our museum visit for the day. That long trip for one painting made it seem very special.

While I lived there, Museum Art School Dean Bill Givler came to NY at least once. He was on a mission for the Art School to hire a painting instructor for a one-year appointment. He knew artists from his early years in NY, and he had leads on others who might be interested in a West Coast jaunt. Remo Ferrugio and Mike Loew were two who he hired on different occasions. While he was visiting, I was pleased to show Bill, my former Dean, what

"Jazz", ink drawing, 1953

I had been doing in my studio in the year since I had left the Art School.

Manuel Izquierdo showed up for two or three weeks. During his stay, he worked on a built-up plaster sculpture of a female figure. Of course, we had many adventures, including getting arrested, or at least getting a ticket, for playing catch with a ball on a nearly deserted beach at Coney Island. We hadn't noticed a sign saying "No ball playing." They took my name, and so I was the defendant when the three of us made the long train ride out there to appear in court. (Money was precious in those days. You didn't just pay the fine and forget it.) We did get the fine reduced, but it was apparent that we were the unwilling paticipants in a municipal money-raising scheme.

On another occasion, Manuel, Don and I rented a rowboat

and rowed out across a huge stretch of bay on Long Island. It was a very hot summer's day. We ate a picnic lunch on a deserted stretch of sandy beach. Don and I stripped naked to go swimming and then spent a couple of hours playing ball. Manuel kept his clothes on, and warned us that we were getting too much sun. The tide turned, and the row back became a very long struggle. Sure enough, by evening, back at the apartment, we realized we each had a terrible case of sunburn. I have never been that burned nor that sick from sunburn.

Don Departs

In October of 1952, Don left for Europe. He decided to use the rest of his GI Bill to travel to Italy and study Italian. He went by boat, and I saw him off one afternoon from the dock in New Jersey. Watching his ship slowly move out of the harbor was a mournful sight. Later, I compensated for it by doing a painting of the scene, but it was a lonesome trip back to Manhattan that day.

Jazz Clubs

Jim Hawkins, an ex-Museum Art School student living in NY, was a jazz musician. We went to jazz clubs, one of which was in the West 50s. It had an arrangement for a half hour national radio hookup on Saturday nights. Even though not that many people were in the audience, the announcer would say "And now live from New York City!" The place was inexpensive enough that even I could afford it (no cover). The jazz was enjoyable and I made sketches there, which I turned into a series of paintings.

Showing My Work

Besides jazz as a subject, what interested me a lot was the street life. There were street dances, women leaning on pillows in windows, street vendors, children playing in the water from open fire hydrants in summer, and families on Coney Island beaches. For an Italian Catholic fair on Mott Street, a gold statue of a saint was carried through the streets, and peopled pinned money to it. Elevated trains rattled by on 3rd and 6th Avenues. You could ride the El all the way up into the Bronx, looking into second story apartment windows all the way. All good stuff for painting.

Showing was not a priority for me then. I felt I needed time to find my way, and showing the work would only force me to solidify a style. I wanted time to develop. But eventually I did feel my prints had a certain consistency, and I took them around to some galleries. The bookstore, Wittenborn, had a viable art gallery, and they were interested in my work. I was given a show of my woodcuts, which I had been doing at my studio, since they could be printed with just spoon pressure on the back of the paper, and I didn't need a press. I showed both black and white and color prints. The show received a small, favorable notice in the Times. Another venue was the Tanager Gallery, where I showed a few small paintings and prints.

Departure

By June of 1953, with my Draft Alternative Service obligation coming up, I packed up my stuff, took paintings off the stretcher bars, and rolled up canvases. I was getting ready to depart New

York. I looked forward to the prospect of doing work camp service in Mexico, and I would have wanted to do it even if it had not been a requirement of the draft. This time I went by plane back to Portland. After crossing the country three times by leg-cramping bus, the plane was a very welcome change.

It was clear to me that I would not return to New York as a place to live. I always knew the West Coast, and specifically Portland, was where I wanted to wind up. For all the richness of New York, I felt that my finishing-school experience there had come to an end.

"Children's Playground," woodcut, 1952

The water filter project, Tlapacoyan, Vera Cruz, Mexico, 1953

Chapter Four

Mexico

Two Years of Alternative Service, 1953-55, I looked forward to working in Mexico with the American Friends Service Committee and to the whole new experience of Mexico itself. The orientation meetings for the work campers took place in Mexico City. Then 15 of us set out in two trucks, heading east 200 miles to one of the work camps in Tlapacoyan, Veracruz.

From a letter I wrote to Don: "Tlapacoyan is a town of about 6,000, with one central school, two churches, and a plaza, where a marimba plays every Sunday evening. The town nestles among hills, which seem to go on forever, hills of the deepest greens, banana trees and oranges and papayas and ferns. The vegetation grows like nothing could stop it. The insects, too, are lush and terribly healthy. This is the country of scorpions, frogs that honk like car horns at night, mosquitos and dragonflies. There are the most beautiful butterflies I have ever seen, and everywhere, circling slowly overhead, black vultures."

The work campers were a mix of young men doing their alternative service, and others, male and female, who were volunteers from many different countries. So, all in all, we were about 20, with a married couple as the group leaders. The housing was a small compound consisting of buildings and a patio, surrounded by an exterior wall. A dorm for the women and one for the men, and common areas for meetings, cooking, and eating. Our residence, the "Casa de Los Amigos," was right in the middle of town, so we had lots of interaction with the local population.

The Quakers do not proselytize, and religious belief was not a requirement to be a work camper. The mission of the work camp was to promote peace through cultural exchange, and to be of service by helping with work projects. Far from imposing anything on the Mexicans, the Friends always tried to arrange things so that they were joining a Mexican project that was already underway. In Tlapacoyan, the women did projects in the town, mostly with women and children, and the men joined an ongoing construction project.

Vultures

Each morning we all gathered in the patio for a half hour of meditation before breakfast. The purpose of the quiet time was to collect one's thoughts for the day. Some read a book, most sat quietly and meditated. The patio was surrounded by a high wall, where vultures came to perch, and stare down at us. No doubt they were contemplating whether these still, quiet, potential morsels were perhaps about to expire.

In the Jungle

The men were helping to construct a water filter that was being built in the jungle about four miles from town. Each morning we traveled by truck as far as the road went. Then we hiked the last mile to the site down a long, narrow trail through the jungle. The filter was being built entirely by hand. Everything had to be carried to the site — rocks, gravel, sand, mortar.

A polluted stream flowed on toward the town. The stream had been temporarily diverted, and we were digging a deep swimming pool shaped depression that was to be filled with large, perforated pipes and covered with stones and gravel. When the stream was diverted back and flowed down into the filter, the water would come out clean enough to drink. That was the hope. We worked alongside the Mexican laborers, digging with pick and shovel. The weather was extremely hot, and it was very hard work. You had to watch that you didn't put your sandaled foot into the opening of an ant hive, as I did one day. And you needed to bring enough personal drinking water. One day we didn't bring enough. We couldn't risk drinking from the stream and that was the only time in my life I experienced excruciating thirst. It lasted only a few hours. But it was a good lesson.

The water filter project lasted another four weeks. On the day when the river was diverted back to its original stream bed and into the filter system, water spilled over the gravel works and down through the pipes. We waited for it to emerge. It looked good, and everyone cheered. Later tests found that the filtering had worked as planned. We felt we had done something really worthwhile. That project turned out to be a great thing for the town.

The Casa de Los Amigos

Back at the Casa in town, people came to visit and children came to do artwork. All of us were giving English lessons. I was working hard to improve my Spanish, and was diligently studying vocabulary. I had taken up with one of the campers, Marione, who was lively and pretty, and who spoke fluent Spanish. She was part Peruvian. We all took part in festivals and dances in the town square. The campers shared the chores and took turns at preparing meals. Two at a time would do the shopping and fix the meals for the day. We held many camp meetings to discuss household matters, or more interesting ones around philosophical questions. The campers were well educated young people, and I found the level of discussion serious and stimulating.

Jaundice

After the second month, I began to feel very tired. I was dragging myself through the day. I also lost my appetite. I was on the cooking detail for Thanksgiving, and we had prepared a really delicious feast. I had baked two pumpkin pies for desert. When everyone sat down to eat, I found I had no appetite at all.

This fatigue and lack of appetite were very worrying. I went to see the local doctor, who examined me, looked at the yellow color under my eyelids, and declared that I had "ictericia." I didn't have enough Spanish to know what that was, and the doctor didn't speak English. But he consulted his Spanish-English dictionary, and declared, "You have the jaundice." What a relief. I had been feeling run down for so long, I was greatly relieved to find out I had something that had a name, and could be dealt with.

Hospital

I left by bus to go to the hospital in Mexico City for treatment.

I was so tired, I could barely drag myself from the bus stop to the hospital building. How good the bed felt! The hospital's diagnosis was that I had infectious hepatitis. Here I was, after only two and a half months in Mexico, flat on my back in a hospital bed. But as it turned out, I was to have plenty of company from my fellow work campers.

One at a time other work campers joined me at the hospital. First Marione, and eventually about 10 others. The hospital stay lasted about three weeks and as we gained strength, we visited each others' rooms. I had a good time drawing portraits of the nurses. They were mostly young, unmarried, and in their 20s. Word got

Second from left: Marione, Tlaxcala, Mexico,1954

around, and they would come and sit for me at the foot of my bed. It was fun, and a great way to work on my Spanish.

Tlaxcala, Tlaxcala

When we were no longer infectious and well enough to leave, the whole recuperating group was sent to a new work camp in Tlaxcala. We were a group of about 12, joining another group of ten healthy campers already there. Tlaxcala was on the desert plateau, hot and dry, and very different from tropical Tlapacoyan. From the Casa, we could see two marvelous mountains, Popocatepetl and Ixtacihuatl. They made magnificent silhouettes as the sun set. At Tlaxcala, fully half the work campers were there to recuperate. Jaundice is very fatiguing, and those who were recuperating could not do much physical work. We did give English classes, did household chores, and I gave art classes to what became a big group of the neighborhood kids. The Friends' main project was road construction, but only a couple of the men were healthy enough for that. The recuperation regimen included lots of rest and lots of brewers yeast tablets. Large jars of these big brown pills sat in the center of the dining room table. We were encouraged to eat as many as possible. They were very malty and quite tasty.

When possible, on weekends we piled into our trucks and went on field trips to the sites of ruins or to the beach. Sometimes we'd scour plowed fields for clay figurines. We found many, most of them quite small. The work camps were not puritan at all. But one requirement was that we not drink alcohol. Drinking could cause undesirable and tricky situations. So it was "nunca tomo"— "I never drink" when drinks were offered. We had two pickup

Kids hanging on to one of our pickup trucks, 1954

trucks at our disposal. One was named "Nunca Tomo" and the other was called "OK Maguey." I lettered the name on the side of the truck with an image of a Maguey plant. Our Mexican friends got a big kick out of the name "OK Maguey."

My lively girlfriend, Marione, was fun most of the time, but she sometimes got into moods of dark depression. We had lots of good times together, and we talked about getting married. It was on again, off again, until we mutually called it off. I'm lucky. It would not have been a success. She went on to marry someone else soon after she left the work camp, and I got to meet her new baby about a year later, before I left Mexico.

Ixmiquilpan, Hidalgo

There were three Quaker work camps in Mexico at that time, the third being in Ixmiquilpan. I was sent there after I had recuperated sufficiently. This town is on the main North-South highway about 100 miles north of Mexico City. It is in the heart of Otomi Indian country, and the Friends' project was to work with the Patrimonio Indijina del Valle de Mesquital, the Otomi Indian agency. The Friends Casa was a large one-story structure consisting of a number of rooms surrounded by a high wall, as were all the Mexican houses. We were right near the center of town, and again we gave classes that brought many visits from the town folk.

We were 24 work campers in all. We were together on the weekends, but during the week we would go in small groups of two or four, to live and work in far-flung Otomi villages up in the hills. We would stay for five days and then return to the Casa at the end of the week. To get to the village I was in, we drove several miles by truck and then hiked more miles into the mountains to a very isolated location. All the Otomies' land was on bare, rocky ground that grew almost nothing. We (two men and two women) lived in a small, two-room stone house. A couple of other stone houses were there, but most of the Otomies lived in huts made of cactus with tin roofs. It was blazingly hot during the day and freezing at night. The Otomies are among the poorest people in the world. No crops would grow there. For income, they depend on fiber spun from the Maguey cactus. Out of this fiber, they weave large bags that are like gunny sacks. These are then sold at market.

They use the milk of the Maguey plant to make pulque, a kind of beer. There are big open barrels of it in the houses; it is the main supplement to their meager diet. Even the children drink it, and by late afternoon everyone in the village is somewhat inebriated. For the most part, they are not belligerent drunks. They did have one small stone building where lime was stored, which also served as a jail, when needed. It would be a very uncomfortable place to stay, because if you move around much, it stirs up the lime dust.

Mostly, the people spoke only Otomi, and no Spanish. The women in our group worked with the Otomi women and children. My partner Tony and I helped rebuild the ruined wall of a small church. I have always loved working with stones and mortar, and this was a very enjoyable project. We worked on that project for the five day stay, and then hiked down a very long trail (four hours) to meet the Friends' truck late on Friday.

Making Slides Shows

After a couple of months of my time in Ixmiquilpan, I began working more closely with the Patrimonio, and particularly, with one interesting man, Raul. He was Otomi, about 35 years old, and a trained anthropologist. The Patrimonio expressed the need to educate the Otomies on health issues, having to do with basic sanitation. Raul and I worked out a series of stories, and I drew illustrations for them. The idea was to make some slide shows to get the message across in an entertaining way. I obtained some blank slide film and made drawings directly on the film. It was exciting to make drawings on such a small scale, and then see them greatly enlarged when projected. The stories involved basic health ideas such as the importance of boiling drinking water. The drawings were in black ink with color added. And they were drawings of people who looked like the Otomies themselves. We hoped they would identify with them so the message might stick.

After we had several slide programs put together, Raul and I set out to visit the far-flung hill villages with our entertainment package. Bear in mind that this was years before the internet, or TV, and the Otomi villages had no electricity, so there was not even radio. We arrived after dark. The two of us were literally the entertainment for the evening, and the whole village turned out. We carried a gasoline-run slide projector, and the whitewashed side of the church (every village had a church) acted as our slide screen. The tiny drawings I had made directly on the slide became huge images on the side of the church.

I had written a script in Spanish (I was quite fluent by this time), and Raul read from it to narrate the script in Otomi. That was all very exciting for me, and it seemed to go over big, with plenty of laughter and comment when we presented the program. Along with the educational stories, I had drawn slides that illustrated a Grimm's Fairy Tale about a woman taking her pig to market. It featured a series of difficulties she encountered along the way and was quite funny. It was the "Looney Tunes" cartoon for the evening. When the show was over, we would be put up for the night in someone's house, and then the next day we moved on to another village. It was our roadshow.

El Salvador

In June 1955, when I had only a couple of months left of my two years of alternative service, I had an opportunity to go to a work camp in El Salvador for the summer. El Salvador was incred-

Educational slide drawings, 1954

ibly verdant; even fence posts stuck in the ground sprouted foliage. It was the rainy season, and heavy rain started at exactly the same time every afternoon. There was very little sun, but a lot of heat. I still often have strong memories of that country, triggered by the smells after certain rainy days here in Portland.

There were two work camps in El Salvador that summer. We were a group of nine in our unit. In a letter to Don I described our work: "Yesterday our group spent the day visiting a UN Demonstration Area. I was considerably impressed with the job they are doing concerning health. The nine of us, some with a little sociology background, most amateurs, are trying to do a social worker's type of job in this village, called Joya de Ceren. It is an experimental housing project, built by the government for formerly landless families. There are communal sugar cane fields, whose profits are going to help people pay for the houses. The five men are helping build chicken coops for the community, and we do some guidance work with the clubs and organizations of the village.

Americans are extremely well accepted in El Salvador. I suspect it's because they have not had the tourists that Mexico has had. It is refreshing to find a general openness, instead of the suspicion of Americans that one often finds in parts of Mexico."

A Scorpion

El Salvador had myriad bugs and insects, including scorpions. Turning over restlessly in my sleeping bag late one night, I felt a sudden jab in my calf. It was as if a nail was hammered into it. As I turned the bag inside out, sure enough, there was a nice big scorpion wagging his tail in the air, then trying to scurry away.

I dispatched it with a shoe. This was before my association with my animal activist later to-be wife. Otherwise, I might have just caught it in a cup and put it outside.

It was scary at the time, because I didn't have any idea how poisonous it might be. Some Salvadorian nurses connected to our work camp lived down the road, and I hobbled to their house and roused them from sleep. They dressed the wound, and reassured me it was the small ones of the species that are the deadly ones. Those the size of my very large scorpion were not as poisonous. So I just had a nice sore, bandaged calf the next day. No real problem.

The Kindness of Strangers

At the end of the summer, I left El Salvador, to head back toward Mexico through Guatemala. I took a small train that wended its way through banana plantations owned by United Fruit, then slowly chugged on up toward Mexico. The train stopped somewhat short of the Mexican border. We passengers disembarked to walk with our baggage along a wooden plank path, through heavy tropical foliage, to the border checkpoint, where we were to meet busses on the other side. I learned from various conversations that to enter Mexico, one was expected to have at least $300 on your person, to show that you were not a vagrant. I had almost no money, and suddenly, it seemed that I might be turned back. I could see myself having to go all the way back to Guatemala City.

But I had been talking with an American family on the train, and when the father understood the situation, he handed me $300 to have in my pocket as we crossed. I have always remembered that as a very generous act. After we got well past the guards, I handed

Phyllis, 1955

it back to him. I was touched by his trust.

I got back to Mexico City, very weary after a long bus ride on uncomfortable seats. After a couple of days of rest at the Casa, I headed north. My two years of alternative service were completed.

Phyllis

On my way back to the United States I stopped off at the Friends Casa in Ixmiquilpan, which was on the main highway. I thought I might just say hello, and stay for a couple of days. Since I'd left in June a whole new group of work campers was there. As was the case before, they were from a variety of countries.

One particular Canadian girl caught my eye. Phyllis Burn-
ham had arrived in Mexico from London, where she had been
living and working for five years. A friend of hers had talked to
her, enthusiastically, about the interesting Quaker work camps in
Mexico, and she had signed up for a six-month period. Phyllis
was movie-star-pretty, with a lively, outgoing personality, and I
was captivated. We got to know each other during those couple of
days, and then I left, ostensibly to return to the United States. But
by that time I had other ideas.

I returned to Mexico City and asked the leader, Ed Duckles,
if I could spend two weeks at Ixmiquilpan, making drawings of
landscape and people. He replied that I couldn't stay there just to

Making adobe bricks, me at left, 1955

make drawings, but if I wanted to join in the work, he would approve that.

I returned to Ixmiquilpan. When I knocked on the door of the Casa, who should answer it, but Phyllis! She had no idea of my devious intentions. "Oh, it's you," she said, and let me in.

The Friends' work project in Ixmiquilpan, at that point, was to help make adobe bricks that would be used for community low-cost housing. We worked with an interesting device into which we shoveled dirt mixed with a sprinkle of cement, and then pulled down on a lever, which compressed it. The resulting block was set out in the sun, to bake into a very strong brick. We made lots of these for the construction stockpile. Both men and women worked together on the project.

Phyllis had a serious boyfriend back in Canada. She was writing him letters. However, I had the advantage of being not in Canada, but close at hand. I saw her every day.

We had a lot in common from the start, including our political and social outlook on the world. At one point, she and I tended to a stray kitten that had been abused. It had been smeared with tar, and Phyllis and I spent a whole afternoon together getting the tar out of its fur. It was a propitious start to our relationship, especially considering what came later: her lifetime of dedicated and productive work in animal welfare.

We made a trip to Mexico City. We went on group picnics. One night, Phyllis and I went with some of the group to a hot springs pool out in the desert. It was a large natural pool, about the size of a municipal swimming pool, with water about chest deep. The desert night air was very cold, the pool waters luxuriantly warm. There were no lights of any kind, except the stars, and

"Las Hermanitas", woodcut, 1956

with the cold air and hot water, the occasion was really magical.

We packed a lot of talking and being together into those two weeks, and at the end of it, I asked her to marry me. Even though I had no money, and no job prospects, she said yes. Phyllis had signed up for the work camp for a six months stint, and had three months more to go. I returned to Portland, and she was to follow in December.

Me, Phyllis, Dr. Francis Newton, Director, Portland Art Museum, 1956

Chapter Five

Back in Portland

Most of my friends were still in Portland, getting on with their lives. I moved in with Manuel for a few days and then rented an apartment in a house on SW Hall Street. I got a job as an assistant to Donald Jenkins, who was then the Art Museum registrar. I liked Donald very much, and he was easy to work with, but I wasn't temperamentally suited to the kind of careful registrar work that needed doing. As it happened, one of the teachers, painter Charles Voorhies, became ill and had to take a leave of absence. The dean, Bill Givler, asked me if I would like to take over his painting class. I did, and I did OK at it, and so began my teaching career at the Museum Art School, which continued for the next 25 years.

I resumed my old life with my old friends. I hadn't told any of them about Phyllis. I don't remember why. Maybe I liked the idea of surprise. I do remember a group of us were at the tavern, a few days before she was to arrive, when I announced: "By the way, I'm getting married on Monday." I remember jaws dropping. I got a kick out of that.

Phyllis Arrives

When Phyllis got off the train in Portland, she wasn't sure if she would remember what I looked like. I didn't have a picture of her, and she didn't have one of me. We did, however, recognize each other right away, and I joyfully took her back to our apartment. In those days, the general public had a more uptight set of morals. I made sure that the landlady knew that the young lady I was bringing to my apartment was my fiancée, and that we were going to be married in a couple of days.

Which we were, on Monday, December 12th, 1955. It took place in the courtroom of a judge who came in especially to do the service. Manuel, my best man, gave the judge, I think, five dollars. Present at the wedding, as witnesses, were Jack and Barbara McLarty, Byron and Doll Gardner, and Manuel. After the ceremony we all went out for a spaghetti dinner. Then Phyllis and I went back to our apartment. We had no thought of going away anywhere for a honeymoon. And we were OK with that.

Our apartment was ten blocks from the art school. I'd hustle home each noon to have lunch with Phyllis, and then hustle back to the school. I was getting lots of exercise. I was making $2400 a year teaching, more money than I'd ever made. But it didn't stretch very far. Later, I bought our first car, a used 1946 Plymouth, for $100. Our bank wouldn't give me a loan for it because I wasn't making enough money. I later used the bank's refusal as an arguing point to get a raise.

The car ran pretty well, when it would start. I kept calling friends for a jump. But I also kept trying to get the last 1/16th inch of wear out of the tires, with the result that I was constantly down on my knees with the jack and tire iron, changing a flat tire. The watchword was always economy.

When I think back on it, I know that it was asking an awful

lot of Phyllis, bringing her to a town where I had very deep, long friendships, and she knew no one. Everyone welcomed her, but a certain amount of time went by before she got used to the rhythm of Portland and our friends, and began to come into her own.

Wayne Morse

The first friend she made, outside of the artists, was Dolores Hurtado. Both of them were volunteers for the Wayne Morse re-election Campaign. Dolores and her husband, Arnold, became our very close friends. He was a young Kaiser doctor, and since they had money, and we didn't, they insisted on paying for anything we did together. They even loaned us their brand new car, so we could drive down to San Francisco for a vacation. I was painting a lot, and I gave them paintings in return.

The Market Street House

After about a year of living in our apartment, we were introduced to Dr. Lendon Smith and his wife, Julie. Rick and Dora Norwood were close friends of the Smiths. "Dunny" Smith was their pediatrician, a humorous and witty person. He later wrote books on child care and nutrition, and became known as "the next Dr. Spock." He was a frequent and popular guest on Johnny Carson's program. Rick and Dora took us to the Smiths' for dinner one night, and Dunny pointed out that the house next door to them was empty. It was owned by their friend, Al Millar, who had been using it to store his mother's furniture for the last three years. They thought he might be willing to sell it. Phyllis and I approached him just as he was beginning to think about it, and we bought it. He was very fond of the house, and somehow he liked us. He had happy memories there and wanted it to go to a couple who would appreciate it and continue to add good vibes.

The house had been left without heat through a very cold winter. Every pipe in the house had frozen and was broken. It had steam radiators, but there was now no heating system and no plumbing. A perfect house for the Johansons. We got the house for $6,600. Al had asked $7,000 but agreed to take less since the plumbing repair would cost $400. Phyllis' generous and wealthy Canadian uncle, who had given each of his nieces and nephews a house, gave us the money to pay for it. Even though we had a lot of work to do on the house, we never had a mortgage, which was, of course, a tremendous help financially.

Nuclear Bomb Tests

I was teaching full time, and Phyllis became more and more active in the community. The cold war raged, and there seemed to be a real possibility of a hot conflict with Russia. Every Monday at noon, the air raid sirens went off, practicing their wail, from a perch high atop a building in downtown Portland.

Nuclear testing was going on above ground, and the poisoning of the atmosphere was more and more evident. Phyllis and I began getting together with Portland's peace groups. We had a number of meetings at our house. As part of those concerns I constructed a booth out of wood and other materials. We took it downtown early on a Monday morning and assembled it against the outer wall of the First National Bank on the corner of 6th and Morrison.

The bank employees became alarmed, and came outside, saying, "You can't put that here against our building." (It was a rather rustic and radical looking structure.) "We have permission from your chairman," we said. Bank chairman EB McNaughton was an influential member of the Portland Art Museum and a great liberal. We marched into the bank and to his office. To the amazement of the staff, he confirmed that he had given us permission to have it there.

"Halt Nuclear Testing," said the banner. The booth was there for a week with mostly women tending it, passing out leaflets, asking people to sign a petition. Phyllis, artist Sally Haley, Do Hurtado and others were there daily. They were a brave lot. Some people agreed with them. Others hurled insults. They were called Communists and worse. That booth was among the first stirrings in Portland of the peace groups that grew larger as time went on.

Pregnant

In 1957, Phyllis became pregnant. In the third month of the pregnancy, she contracted mumps from a visit to Manuel's house where one of his kids had it. Phyllis' doctor took me aside and told me there was a good chance that the fetus would be malformed. She didn't recommend an abortion. (It was not legal back then.) I took in the news but I didn't think too much about it until much later.

On a car trip to Seattle to visit my folks, Phyllis began to feel a great pulling in her abdomen at every slowing or stopping of the car. She had a miscarriage soon after we got to Seattle. My mother had had a couple of miscarriages and was a great help to Phyllis. The fetus was about an inch long, a boy. It had tiny hands, pro-

Aaron, Phyllis, 1958

portionate with his body, with tiny, tiny fingers. Being the curious fellow that I am, I thought it would be interesting to preserve it. I put it into a jar with formaldehyde, but after a few days it turned whitish and looked rather grizzly. We didn't keep it.

Pregnant Again 1958

Phyllis' second pregnancy resulted in a beautiful baby boy. In those days you didn't know, until the birth, whether it would be a boy or a girl. And during delivery, no one thought the father might be allowed in the delivery room. Phyllis' labor lasted about five hours, and all I could do was drink coffee and smoke cigarettes in the waiting room. Eventually the nurse came out, to announce, "You have a baby boy and he is complete and healthy." I suddenly started to tear up. I was not quite aware of how much intense emotion had been locked up during this experience until that moment.

Aaron Adam. We picked the names because we liked them, not thinking about honoring any relatives. We found out later that my father's sister Ida, who we had very little contact with, thought we had picked the name Aaron to spite her. Her soldier husband Aaron had left her for a French woman at the end of WWII. I hadn't made that connection at all. My mother tried to reassure my aunt that it had nothing to do with her Aaron. With what success, I'm not sure.

Our Dada Show 1961

Inspired by a big Dada show in New York that year, Jack McLarty got the idea to do such a show in Portland. He asked me to help organize it. We got together about 20 artists who were enthusiastic about doing some pieces outside their usual way of working and in the spirit of Dada. We obtained the loan of the "Bishops House," a privately owned building on SW 2nd and Stark. It was going to be renovated but was presently empty. We took over the whole second floor, and our show ran for four weeks. What a show it turned out to be!

Some of the participating artists were: Louie Bunce, Mike Russo, LaVerne Krause, Manuel Izquierdo, Jon Colburn, and Jay

At the Dada show, from left: Jack McLarty, Manuel Izquierdo, me, Jay Backstrand, 1961

Backstrand. All of them made pieces especially for the show. A large dining table held various strange items: a meat grinder that seemed to be spitting out body parts, a birdcage containing "dynamite," and a centerpiece I made, a plaster cast of Phyllis' bare behind resting on a platter with a garnish of play money.

The main room had two fireplaces with large mantels. We made plaster life masks of each other to hang on the mantels. An old leather rocker formed into an "electric chair." Many pieces were raunchy, suggestive, and anti-religious. Jon Colburn made a construction composed of bedpans and other such medical devices. It

"Cleanliness Is Next To Godliness," Jon Colburn, assemblage, 1961

was accompanied by a recording of Jon's voice, repeating over and over, "Cleanliness is next to Godliness." As he read, the inflection varied and became nauseous and retching by the end. Besides the bite and satire in the pieces, many of them were hilariously funny.

Portland had a vice squad in those years, and as we were setting up the show we were honored by a visit from a couple of members of the plain clothes squad. "If it was up to me, I'd close the show down right now!" one of them said. But even in those

Cast of Phyllis' behind, plaster, table center piece, Dada show, 1961

days, authorities were cautious about seeming to censor artists. The show went on, and was very popular. We had a couple of different openings. LaVerne dressed as a witch and rode a stationary bicycle at one of them. There was a panel discussion, completely in the Dada spirit. Dr. Smith gave a funny lecture on bedwetting, during which Manuel ostentatiously excused himself to go to the bathroom. Poet Ken Hanson, of Reed College, read the Chinese alphabet. After a minute and a half of silence, he declared, "There is no alphabet in Chinese."

At the end of the run of the show, we held an auction where anyone could acquire the exhibits cheap. After which, all the leftovers were tossed down a chute, into a dumpster. It was a fitting end to our Dada show. Many of the life masks, however, survived. I kept the ones of Louie Bunce and myself.

New Galleries

Two new galleries opened in Portland in 1961. They were the first serious commercial enterprises for exhibiting regional art. Up to that time, there had been practically no galleries in Portland. Aside from the Karouba, which was partly a gift shop, the only showing places were restaurants and a few college galleries. But then things began to change.

Jack and Barbara McLarty started the Image Gallery, and Arlene Schnitzer opened the Fountain Gallery. Most working artists joined one or the other of them. I went with the Image Gallery. It was on the ground floor of a large, older house on NW 25th and Overton. Many of the artists joining the Image Gallery helped with installing and painting walls. Jack continued to teach a full schedule, paint in his studio, and organize shows at his gallery at the same time. He was about 42. What energy one has at that age!

I showed there for about eight years until I felt I needed a change, and left to be on my own. Later I showed at other galleries. I was with the Sally Judd Gallery for several years, until she closed. Then the Fountain Gallery, until they closed. Then the Lawrence Gallery for several years, until they closed, followed by

Elizabeth Leach and Pulliman Deffenbaugh, and for a brief time with Mark Woolley. Now I show with Augen Gallery, where I have been for the past ten years.

Drinking

All through my early and middle years in Portland, the artist community was heavily immersed in alcohol. This was certainly true of artists in New York and in many other artist communities. It was an integral part of the artists' culture.

In Portland, all through the 50s and 60s, there were regular parties, every week or two, that included most of the artists. These were hosted by one or another of us, taking turns. Phyllis and I had countless parties at our house. They were lots of fun, with music and dancing, and inventive games. Phyllis loved getting involved in the planning. She amassed a huge collection of hats, mostly from the Goodwill. There were fifty or sixty of them. They were great for giving you permission to look ridiculous. There were acrobatic games, some of them competitive (trying to jump over a broomstick, held between your own outstretched hands). We placed a bolt in the central beam of the living room, from which we hung a rope with a flat plywood seat, and people could swing back and forth, narrowly missing onlookers. We spent hours writing fortunes and putting them into empty peanut shells glued back together, "You are a distant relative of Van Gogh, and your right ear is feeling itchy."

Almost none of us used pot or any other substances, just alcohol. Manuel, high on wine, like the rest of us, was very entertaining. He would get going with stories and improvisations, carrying on with a small group long after the main party had left. Sometimes until 4 a.m. On one occasion, the remaining six or seven people at the party decided that we should go for a walk to Washington Park. When we were outside, Manuel started loudly singing some Spanish street song. I had to tell him, "Hey, tone it down. The neighbors are sleeping."

The parties were pretty wild. At one of our New Year's parties, we were serving red wine punch out of a very large plastic bowl, about 36 inches in diameter. It sat on a low table. Late in the evening, one of our female friends decided to take a bath in the punch bowl, fully clothed. She was just settling in when it tipped, and a sea of red wine sloshed out over the carpet. We all thought it was hilarious. At another party, a couple was dancing on our spindly legged coffee table, which broke. I fixed it, and then we encouraged dancing on it again at a later party, with the same results. At still another party, this time at Bill Givler's, a couple danced on top of their grand piano. It did not break, though Nell Givler was a bit horrified.

A New Year's Eve party at artists Ray and Hazel Chilstrom's could have resulted in a disaster, when two of the inebriated guests decided to have a pretend duel with real foils that had been hanging, as decoration, over the fireplace. The sharp points were not corked and one of the participants got a foil run clear through his thigh. That stopped the swordplay, and he was rushed to the hospital. He was eventually OK, and luckily it didn't do any permanent damage.

Parties were lots of fun, and cathartic, but along with all that drinking, people drove home when they were in no condition to drive. We were all very lucky.

I drank too much, along with everyone else. I also drank every evening, and a hangover was an ever-present reality in the mornings. I was dependent on having some wine every day. In the back of my mind, always as a caution, was my father's family and their alcoholism. A couple of times, over the years, I stopped drinking. Sometimes for as long as a year or two. Then I'd slowly get back into it. Finally, in January of 2013, I decided I had reached my lifetime quota of alcohol. In my fantasy, a ledger exists somewhere that allots me a certain lifetime amount. So, having had my full allotment, I stopped drinking. I sometimes miss the buzz and freedom of attitude that drinking brings. But otherwise, I don't think about it. It is now simply not a part of my identity, as it once so intimately was.

Smoking

The same is true for smoking, though that was finished for me long ago, the summer of 1963. Back in the days when I smoked, I could not picture myself without a cigarette. How could I have a cup of coffee without my cigarette? I simply didn't see how I could be myself. I was smoking two packs a day. Every day. I stopped because I began to get severe pains in my chest. That really scared me. I could have gone to the doctor to find out what was causing the pains. But I didn't have to get an expert opinion to confirm it was the cigarettes. So I just stopped.

Fred Meyer happened to be having a sale on three-pound bags of raw cashews. The sale went on for a couple of weeks. They became my erstwhile companion in the studio. My mouth needed constant attending to. I would sit there not working, just look-

ing at the unfinished painting and shoveling in the cashews. After about a week, most of the cigarette craving was gone. But the
cashews, and extra eating, went on for a long time. When I went
back to school that fall, at the first faculty meeting, I was greeted
with "What happened to you?" I was at least 20 pounds heavier.
But I had conquered the smoking. I was very happy about that.

My studio, early 1960s

Poster for my Portland Art Museum show, 1966

Chapter Six

London

In 1965, I took my first sabbatical leave from the school, and we rented out our house to a family who agreed to look after our cats while we were gone. Then Phyllis, Aaron and I set out for London for the year. Phyllis had worked in London for several years before we were married and loved the city. We stayed in a hotel for the first week while we searched newspapers for a decent, not too expensive place to live. We found a great place on the ground floor of a three-story building on Holland Park Road. This consisted of two very large rooms with very high ceilings. The front room served as the living room, kitchen, and Aaron's bedroom and the back room served as our bedroom, and my studio.

This worked out very well, but I decided right away that it would be intolerable to combine oil-turpentine fumes and sleeping. So I switched from oil to acrylics, which I had not used before. This gave me a new outlook on painting, because of the speedy drying time, and the flatness the medium seemed to call for. There was a large wall to hang the painting on while working, and since I was going to be rolling the paintings to take them back to the States at the end of the year, I decided I would forego stretcher bars and simply stretch the canvas on the wall. Stretching canvas on the wall had two effects: the scale could be very large, and it induced me to try some shapes other than the usual rectangle. Because the painting wasn't on stretcher bars, I could play with the shape, or change it, according to how it was working with the painting.

Sleeping in the same room with my paintings meant when I woke up during the night, the unfinished painting stared down at me offering suggestions to my partly-awake self. Seeing the work in half-light like that offered a nice, semiconscious meditation.

Holland Park

Aaron, seven years old, was assigned to St. Mary Abbot's grade school. He was just old enough to be in the top year of students there, and that made it a lot easier, I think, for him to fit in. The school was located straight across Holland Park from where we lived, about eight blocks or so. Phyllis and I, or sometimes both of us, walked Aaron to school in fog-shrouded lanes. Peacocks roamed freely. London was noisy, and polluted with smelly exhaust fumes, but a block or so into the park, all the noise and pollution dissipated. That huge park is used for all sorts of activities. Those were very beautiful, fairytale, walks. On one of the sunny days, when the three of us walked in the park, we came upon an area cordoned off for movie filming. Lo and behold, there was Michael Caine — they were shooting a scene for "Alfie."

I was looking for a place to make prints in London. Asking around at one of the art museums, I happened to talk to a young woman who was an assistant at the only privately run workshop in London available to printmakers on a daily basis. Birgit Skiold, a Swedish expat, ran it. The workshop was located in the basement of a building on Charlotte Street owned by Adrian Heath, a well known British painter. Birgit named the workshop, appropriately enough, "The Basement." You would go through the front door, along a short narrow hallway, and try not to scrape your shoulder against a large David Hockney painting ("Berlin") hanging there. The painting belonged to Mr. Heath. Birgit was a gregarious person, an artist-printmaker, who made The Basement available to artists for long periods or short ones, and for a very modest fee. She was acquainted with all sorts of artists. Many of the bigger names in English art made prints in her facility. Even though it was a far cry from being fancy, or even very neat (inky-fingered blotters), it had a good size etching press, a litho press, and all the other equipment you needed to get the job done.

I settled in to do etchings a couple of days a week. I got to be good friends with Birgit and met a number of interesting artists, some of whom came for only a day or two, others for several months. Like all print workshops, it was a good place to discuss ideas and gain new techniques and methods from other printmakers. I learned a lot, all of which served to refresh my visual language that year.

Hockney

David Hockney was among the artists Birgit knew. In 1966, he was just beginning to be widely known. Birgit asked if I would like to visit him. Of course, I would. He was living in a second-floor flat in a brick building. There are published photos of him walking in front of it. We went there one afternoon.

He was working on sketches for sets for Ubu Roi, which were spread around the floor of one of the cleared-out bedrooms he

"Teatime for Three Nudes," acrylic, 1966

used for studio space. Juan Miro had done sets for Ubu in the past, and Hockney told us that Miro had come around for a visit to see what Hockney was doing with it. "He pulled up in a limousine, and he was a tiny figure of a man," he said. I don't remember what he said about Miro's reaction. But Hockney seemed quite bemused by a visit from the great Spanish painter.

He brought out a portfolio of "The Rakes Progress," his recently finished series of 16 etchings, and laid them out on a bed to show them to us. One had coffee stains on it which he said he himself had spilled.

Hockney was a very sociable guy, so I was bold enough to call him up the next day to see if I could return and take a few pictures of his work to share with my classes back home. He agreed, and I went back and took a number of slide photos. We sat and talked for a while over a cup of coffee. He said that he thought of himself not so much as a painter but as an image maker, (which I think is still true.)

Swimming

Aaron and I often went swimming at one of the municipal swimming pools that were maintained by the city of London. They were cavernous places, with very tall ceilings and booths for changing along the side of the pool. The water was chilly, and the whole thing had a very 19th century feel about it. I got a lot of inspiration for paintings from those swimming sessions.

I enrolled in a night class in judo. The teacher was a black belt, a white guy in his early 60s. I had always thought I should do some contact sport like that, and now at age 38, I tried it out. It was arduous and enlightening. We learned to do some throws and also how to fall. At the end of several weeks of sessions, I went from a white to a yellow belt, one small step up the ladder toward black belt. I was not that good, but it did give me some satisfaction as an accomplishment. At the end, the teacher gave the group a rousing talk; he had arranged for our group to challenge one from another club next year. That excited the class, and I was excited along with them. I learned something about myself I wasn't aware of — the excitement of identifying with a strong group force that impels you along with it. That brief experience gave me a visceral sense of how a crowd gets riled up.

The next judo sessions were to take place after a Christmas break. I didn't sign up for them. They were just too much hard work. I had learned what I wanted from them. I wanted to save my energy for prints and painting.

I did a lot of painting that year, which resulted in a show at the Portland Art Museum on our return home. It was titled "London and After." They were big paintings, many of them shaped canvases of bathers, and mythological scenes.

London Again

Three years later I took an unpaid leave from teaching, and we returned to London for another year's stay. This time I had a grant from Art Advocates, a Portland organization that sponsored artists so they could take a year away from their regular jobs to concentrate on producing a body of work. The set up was this: a group, in my case 30 people, put up a certain amount of money and in return received artwork at the end of the year. I proposed a portfolio of ten etchings, for which each participant put up $200. What a bargain — but then again this was back in 1969. As a result of the grant, I had $6,000 to live on for the year. Not only did it pay the airfare for the three of us, it was enough to rent an apartment on Queens Gate Terrace, near Albert Hall, a great location, and food and other necessities for the whole year.

Our apartment was on the top floor of a five-story building. No elevator. All the food and other supplies had to be carried up the 100 stairs (we counted them). And the garbage, and anything else, had to be carried down.

Aaron was 11 years old that year. He walked and took the bus to school on his own. London seemed safe. His school was another matter. It was a tough school in a working-class part of town. He was not among the oldest students, as he had been on our first London trip. He had to endure some bullying, and the instructional level was not very good. But he survived it.

At one point Aaron entered a contest put on by an ice cream company. The object was to invent and draw a super hero's vehicle. He did a very inventive drawing, and lo, and behold, he won a top prize, which was a Raleigh bicycle. He was thrilled with it and rode it around on the wide sidewalks near where we lived. Then, so that it wouldn't get stolen, he carried it up the 100 stairs to our apartment, and then, all the way down to ride the next day. And this was not a lightweight bicycle!

Brass Rubbings

Phyllis got interested in doing brass rubbings, and spent many days taking the bus out to small towns, where there was a church with an engraved brass that was available for rubbing. Most of the sites have been off limits for rubbing for a long time now, because of wear and tear on the brasses, but in 1969, many were still available. You'd pay a small fee, and tape your paper down to the floor over the brass engraving. Then with a black "heel ball," like a big crayon, you'd go back and forth over the surface until the image became clear and strong. Heel balls come in grades from hard to soft. The best and clearest rubbing is made with the hard ball and with lots of patient rubbing to get a sharp image. Phyllis did quite a few rubbings. The image is generally a figure in armor with an animal at his feet. I did an etching, a take-off of that subject, which was a full-length self-portrait with a dog at my feet.

On the way to the bus we often passed a pet store near our apartment. A fruit bat was in the window. There it hung, upside down, enclosed in its folded wings. Phyllis was very fond of bats (we belong to Bat Conservation International) and she would stop to admire this one whenever we passed it. I incorporated an image of that fruit bat into one of the etchings I did for my Art Advocate series.

The Basement Again

With the grant obligation in hand, I returned to Birgit's Basement workshop. This time I was there nearly every day, since I had a set number of works that needed to be completed. I did about 20 different prints during that year, a good thing, because I was able to choose from those the ten I needed for the portfolio. I worked a set number of hours each day, and took the #9 double-decker bus back to our Queens Gate apartment at around 6 p.m. Birgit and others working at the workshop were fascinated with the idea that I was making prints that had already been paid for.

Warrington Colescott was in London making prints that year. He is the brother of painter Bob Colescott, and did wonderful, satirical, intaglio prints. He was a friend of Birgit's. I got to know him, he was a very sweet guy. He had a car, and on several occasions he went way out of his way to give Phyllis and me a lift home after a party.

Adrian's Close Call

Adrian Heath, who owned the building that housed Birgit's shop, had his studio on the main floor. Adrian was a very good painter. His paintings were abstract but had a sense of figure in them, as well. His studio door was often open, at the end of the hall, and as you went down to the workshop, you could see his partly finished painting on the easel. He would often come downstairs to see what was going on, to sit and talk. He was a man in his 50s, who was short and a bit stocky. He had been a belly gunner on a bomber during the war. You had to be small to fit into the belly turret. One day he told us a harrowing story, about his plane getting shot up on a raid over Germany, about being trapped in his turret, with twisted steel surrounding him. The plane was able to limp back toward England, losing altitude all the time. They were going to have to make a belly landing, no wheels. One of the crew managed to get a small axe to Adrian. He barely had room to move his arms; he had to try to chop himself loose, and get out of the turret, before the plane crash landed. It was a long descent, and if he couldn't get free, he would be crushed on landing. He made it out just in time. The war was still very fresh in the minds of Londoners, even at the end of the 60s.

Aaron Leaves Early

William Lapham, a boyhood friend of Aaron's, came from Portland to stay with us for the month of May. School was not yet out for Aaron, but we thought he had had enough of that school (academically he wasn't learning much), and we pulled him out.

"Juxtaposition, Four Figures," intaglio print, 1970

He and William got to have fun together for a whole month. Then we sent the two of them back to Portland to stay with William's family while Phyllis and I had a month to ourselves in London and Paris. It turned out to be one of the sweetest times we ever had together. Something like a second honeymoon.

Printing The Plates

After returning to Portland, I had to produce the prints for the portfolios. The prints were to be in editions of 30, and I didn't want to spend my time in London finishing editions (rather tedious, time-consuming work), so I made a proof of each print and waited until we returned to Portland to deal with the printing. The editions entailed making ten editions of 30, or in other words 300 prints. These were not small, simple, plates. They were 18x24 inches, and each one involved color and some complicated plate structure. I decided to devote two days a week to the printing and spread it out over a few weeks. I enlisted Phyllis to help with the wiping of the plates. I taught her some techniques, and she did a very good job at it. We had an enjoyable time, completing the editions together. I made portfolios for them, and all the sponsors seemed happy with their prints. One portfolio went to the Coos Art Museum, another went to the Chicago Art Institute.

I also brought back from London a group of prints by contemporary British printmakers, that I had gathered together with Birgit's help, and a show of these occurred at the Portland Art Museum: "British Prints Today." The prints were then donated by the artists to the museum collection. A useful way to spread one's prints to good venues around the world.

One of our film brochures, 1973

Chapter Seven

Printmaking Films

Manson Kennedy was a young, handsome photographer who looked a little like Warren Beatty. He had recently returned (1970) to Portland from Kansas City. We got to be friends, and he decided he wanted to document my work. One thing led to another, and we decided to make a film on intaglio printmaking techniques. I was teaching printmaking, along with painting and drawing, and I discovered that there were no contemporary films on intaglio processes. "Let's make one." How innocently some plans begin.

A year and several thousand dollars later, we had a 38 minute, 16 mm color film titled "Etching and Color Intaglio, A Close Up of the Medium." It went on to win the Golden Eagle award for the best educational film of 1972. We marketed it ourselves, with a direct mailing to college art departments around the country, and eventually it was rented or purchased, by over 100 college art departments.

Manson and I worked closely on the planning and the content. We set each other off creatively, with all kinds of ideas. Everything seemed so fertile, working with Mans. We felt free enough with each other to speculate on crazy and funny concepts. When we were working upstairs in my studio, Phyllis, downstairs, would often hear peals of raucous laughter.

Filmmaker Manson Kennedy, 1972

Mans and I had a ball making the film. He was from a family with money, and he purchased a brand new, 16 mm movie camera. The editing had to be done by physically cutting and splicing, hanging strips of film on a clothes line. Mans was a kind of genius. He was a still photographer and had not made a film before. He was reading a how-to-do-it book on filmmaking while putting together a film that would later win a top award.

We took the film to New York to show it around. One venue was an evening showing at the Museum of Modern Art for a sizable group of printmakers and other interested parties. Karl Schrag came to it, as did Una Johnson, the print curator at the Brooklyn Art Museum. We got some good endorsements from that trip.

"Printmaker"

Three years later, Mans and I made another film. The United States Bicentennial was coming up, and grant money was available through the National Endowment for the Arts, for each of the States to produce art projects for the bicentennial year. We were awarded one of the grants. Our proposal was to make a half hour film which highlighted the art of seven Oregon printmakers, with segments of about four minutes each. They included John Rock, Jack McLarty, Manuel Izquierdo, LaVerne Krause, Jim Hibbard, Louie Bunce and myself. We wanted the film to show the major printmaking mediums, as well as some of the reasons and motivations for making prints. The film is called "Printmaker." Both this film and "Etching and Color Intaglio" were later issued together on a DVD.

The Watergate

Phyllis and I made a trip to Washington DC around this time, and stayed at the Watergate with Irma and her husband, former Portland neighbors, who lived there. Irma had previously worked at NPR, and had been Susan Stamberg's boss when Susan was just starting out in radio. She invited Susan and her husband to dinner. Susan, who has a lot of background in the arts, is as warm and unpretentious as you would expect from her radio persona.

An Inky Butt

That trip to Washington was a chance to drop in on a young

printmaker I had corresponded with, who was teaching high school students, on Saturdays, at the Smithsonian. He didn't know I was in town, but I enquired at the front desk, and was told that his classroom was downstairs in one of the basement rooms. Walking down the corridor, Phyllis and I looked around a door, into a room, and there he was. "George?!" He had just finished showing the "Printmaker" film to his class, and had turned the lights back on, when one of the "stars" of the film appeared out of the blue. Magic!

We stepped into the room, and he introduced us. It was the printmaking studio, and as we were standing there, Phyllis backed up against an inky table, and her light, cream colored dress suddenly had a black smudge on her butt. They got us a little hand solvent, and I proceeded to wipe away at the spot. So not only had I magically appeared at the end of the film, but five minutes later, I was wiping away at Phyllis' bottom in front of the class. What a piece of performance art.

"The Portland Three"

During spring break in 1972, Louie, Manuel, and I made a trip to New York. We were invited to stay with Rose Slivka, who owned a nice, three-story building in the East Village. Rose was editor of Craft Horizon magazine, and had been married to sculptor David Slivka. Louie had not been to New York for quite a while, but he had a lot of artist friends there. As we went around to various functions and bars, we became known as the "Portland Three." (This was around the time of the antiwar group known as the Chicago Eight.) We did a lot that week. Besides visits to art

de Kooning at work, Springs, Long Island, New York, 1972

museums we had access to many parties and studios through Rose and Louie.

Zero Mostel attended one party and Manuel, always full of charm, was trying to persuade him to come out west and give a talk at the Museum Art School commencement. He seemed interested, though it never actually came about.

Rose was renting out her basement two-room apartment, which had a separate entrance, to John Lennon and Yoko Ono. It was not general knowledge that they lived there, although a few teenage girls had somehow found out, and from time to time left small bunches of flowers at the door. I must confess to following suit in a way. One day, early on a Sunday morning, as we were leaving the building, I saw that the New York Times was still at their doorstep. So I took out a pen, and wrote on the top margin, "Greetings from Aaron Johanson," just so I could tell Aaron about it later.

deKooning

Rose knew a lot of artists, and Louie was renewing old acquaintances, whom he had not seen for years. Bill deKooning was one he had known in his early days in New York. Rose arranged for the four of us to drive out to his place in Springs, Long Island, to pay him a visit. We rented a small car, and piled into it for the two and a half hour trip.

The house/studio, which deKooning had built to his specifications, is quite well known from published photographs. It sits on acreage in a woodsy area. As we drove up to it, we could see him through the glass facade, working on a painting which was hanging on the painting wall.

One of his assistants let us in, and he came to greet us. I had known deKooning, and had seen him at parties, when I lived in New York, but there was no reason for him to remember me, since I was just a young kid of 20 at the time. He looked, and sounded, just the same. He had a strong, and attractive, Dutch accent. He was not drinking at the time; I think he had been on the wagon for a couple of years. Someone brought coffee in huge coffee cups, and we sat in oversize, handsome rocking-chairs.

I asked if I could take some pictures, and he said, "Go ahead. This place has been photographed so much already." So I wandered around, taking as many photos as I pleased. He was doing

The floor slot, de Kooning studio, 1972

sculptures, as well as painting, and there were several plywood and metal armatures, some with clay on them, some waiting. Certain areas of the vast studio had large charcoal line drawings spread out, helter-skelter, on the floor. There were dozens of bowls full of paint, mixed with Safflower oil. He liked this medium because it dried so slowly, and left the paint malleable for a long time.

One interesting feature of the studio was a slot cut in the floor, parallel to the painting wall. This allowed a large painting to be lowered down a couple of feet into the floor, making it possible for him to work on the top of the painting without climbing up on a step ladder.

The canvas he was working on was one of the later woman figures, all chaos, and high-pitched color. Pieces of newspaper were pressed into the wet paint in places that would probably be pulled off later. Five or six other paintings in progress, leaned against the

From left: Louie, Rose Slivka, de Kooning, Manuel, 1972

wall, all looking pretty similar.

On the second floor, a catwalk was suspended above the painting area. I went up there, looked down, and it was very impressive. From there you got a great, long, view of the painting wall and the whole work area.

deKooning took a phone call from his old friend, Adolph Gottlieb, who was in the hospital, seriously ill. Then Louie talked for a long time to deKooning about PCVA, the Portland Center for Visual Art, hoping to get him to think about having a show there, and coming out to Oregon for a talk. Wouldn't that have been grand? But deKooning was about 70 at that time and not inclined to do more traveling. So that was not in the cards.

He was a very open person, interested in all kinds of visual expression. He was curious about anything visual. He told us about looking in on an amateur art exhibition there in Springs and being absorbed by the earnestness of one or two of the paintings. He appreciated some qualities in the work, of which the painters themselves were possibly unaware.

Lee Krasner

We were invited to go to dinner at Lee Krasner's apartment. Louie had known both Pollock and Krasner in the early New York days. In fact, it was Louie who first took Lee to visit Pollock's studio, and introduced them. Pollock had been dead for 25 years by the time of our visit, and Krasner was living in a fancy Manhattan apartment building with a doorman. The elevator man took us up to her floor. He waited conspicuously until she opened the door to us, to make sure we were legitimate. It was a roomy apartment, a conventional structure, not a loft. She maintained her studio in one of the rooms. The apartment walls held some small Pollock paintings as well as some of her own work. There was much talk of the old days, between her and Louie.

Louisiana

In 1972, Jack Wilkenson, formerly head of the art department at University of Oregon, and then head of the art department at Louisiana State University, asked me to fill in for a semester for printmaker James Burke, who was going on a half year sabbatical.

I took a one term leave from the Art School. We made arrangements for Aaron to stay in Portland, and with a loaded-up station wagon, Phyllis and I drove south. In Baton Rouge, the beginning of September was very hot, with high humidity. We got an apartment a few blocks from the University. Our apartment was air-conditioned. So was the school. But not our car. The heat outside was stifling.

I had never been in the South before and didn't know what to expect. LSU seemed fairly liberal, a racial mix of students in which minorities seemed to be accepted. As it is with University art departments, many of the students were taking the art class not out of their great interest in art, but to fulfill a requirement or get an easy credit. But a fair number of serious students made the teaching worthwhile. The campus was big and home to hundreds of bicycles.

In the class, I was able to introduce some new techniques and approaches. And I think what I brought seemed fresh to the students. I taught two days a week, and had the rest of the time to draw and paint. I was also in the midst of working on the script for the etching film Mans Kennedy and I were making.

Bourbon Street

We wanted to go down to New Orleans, about 80 miles south, to take in the jazz scene. We started out on a boat trip down river which made several stops on the way. Phyllis and I had to get off at the first stop because the heat was too oppressive to go on. About six weeks later the weather cooled somewhat, so we were able to drive to New Orleans. Bourbon Street was pretty wonderful. Just walking down the street in the evening, passing clubs with open doors and windows, you'd hear great jazz flowing out of one club after the other. For all the fame of the Preservation Hall Jazz Band, the room they played in was quite a small space. On the night we went there, all the seats were full. The eight-piece band was sitting on a low podium, getting ready to play. One of the players saw that we didn't have seats. He invited us to sit on an old trunk to one side of the bandstand, and we did, more or less right in with the band. It was a grand night with great music!

Nixon vs McGovern

The presidential election of '72 was coming up, and Phyllis became a volunteer for the McGovern campaign. The Democratic party was fairly small in Louisiana, and I remember our going to an evening Democratic Party function at someone's house on a beautiful warm evening. The group was meeting outside in a walled garden. I had the thought that someone could easily lob a bomb over the wall, and destroy most of the state's Democrats in one swoop. We met some interesting people through Phyllis' volunteer work. But Louisiana voted to re-elect Richard Nixon, right on cue.

"Easy Rider"

A movie theater in the old part of town was near the Mississippi levee. One afternoon I went there to see "Easy Rider," which I had not seen before. The film ends with the deaths of the two motorcyclists, shot by a couple of ne'er-do-wells as the riders cruise down the levee road by the Mississippi. The cyclists are left sprawled out dead on the road. I came out of the theater, into the bright afternoon sunshine, and as I looked down the street, I saw the exact stretch of road where they had filmed that scene. A nice bit of spookiness.

Football

Jack Wilkenson had an extra ticket for a big football game. At LSU they are all big. The team was playing the University of Oregon. It was a night game as all of them were at that time. Our seats were at the very top row of a very large bowl, which held about 80,000 people. Brilliantly lit inside the stadium and coal black above the top edge it seemed like a gigantic spaceship. And the roar of the crowd was like huge rocket engines. The school mascot was a real tiger, kept in a small cage and wheeled out for the games. I hope that terrible bit of cruelty has long since been retired.

It was a good game, but the University of Oregon lost.

Jack's Dog

Wilkenson was a good painter who worked in oil, painted figuratively, and used very broad forms. When I visited his studio, he had a bunch of recent paintings, unstretched, lying face up on the floor. He also had a big Dalmatian, who came romping into the studio, trotting all over the paintings. I was alarmed. But Jack said "Oh it's alright. My paintings are tough, they can take it. No problem." Jack was bald, he drove a small Volkswagen, and his dog sat in the back behind him, resting his chin flat on top of Jack's head. It was as if the dog guided him on where to go. On a long trip, the dog and Jack were content to stay exactly like that, mile after mile. He had a dog for a hat.

Hollywood Beckons

Somewhere around 1977, our friends Ed and Sandy Martin invited Manuel, Phyllis, and me down to Los Angeles to stay with them for a week. They have a nice ranch-style house with several bedrooms at the top of the hill on Mulholland Drive. The house is built in an L shape, facing a modest-size swimming pool. From the pool area, we look far down toward Hollywood studios and a vast landscape of buildings, stretching toward the North as far as the eye can see—at least until the smog obscures the horizon. It is a particularly impressive and breathtaking view at night, when you are standing on the diving board taking in that vast carpet of lights.

Ed and Sandy are very generous people, and we have been their weeklong guests a couple of times. Ed is a cinematographer, and Sandy is a producer, working mostly on commercials. They have lots of contacts in "the industry," and they arranged a tour of Warner Brothers studios in a limousine driven by Jack Warner's private chauffeur. Ed and Sandy didn't go along. So it was just Manuel, Phyllis, and myself. What fun that was! The car had tinted windows so that it was not easy to see inside, and we found, as we were driven around the lot, that actors and others who recognized the car, were peering at us, wondering what important visitors were inside.

The Warner Brothers studios are located on a huge plot of 62 acres. We drove around for a while, and then got out to explore on our own, to be picked up later. Visitors are not allowed to take pictures, particularly unaccompanied, as we were. But I hadn't seen the sign forbidding it, so I just clicked away whenever something interesting struck me. I think, because in my ignorance I was so brazen about it, everyone assumed I had permission. No one told me to stop. Many sets from various movies strung out one after the other. A western set would be only a short distance from the set of a London street. The set with the house for "The Waltons" was one of them. I took a picture of Manuel sitting on the Waltons' steps, with Phyllis on his lap. We wandered around, and then had lunch in the commissary, which was full of actors, some in their working costumes.

The dress is sloppy-casual among film people, and I guess my having a gray beard, Levis, and open collar shirt meant that I looked as if I could be a director or producer. Along came Lorne Greene, and as he passed us, he nodded to me, and said, "How are you? Nice to see you again."

When Manuel was off doing something else, Phyllis and I wandered on to a set where they were filming "California Suite." In a mock-up of a bedroom, Maggy Smith and Michael Caine were doing the scene where they arrive home after an evening out. Only the interior of the room was finished off. The outside was raw plywood. Phyllis and I stood outside one of the windows to watch. We had a clear view, and were presumably out of camera range, because no one asked us to move. So we watched a couple of takes of a scene where they enter the room, and Maggy Smith comes toward "our" window, and tosses her coat on the bed. When I look at that scene in the movie now, I know that George and Phyllis are standing there, outside that window, like ghosts, just out of view.

"18 People in 14 Paintings"

In 1976, I had a show of my large-scale portrait paintings at the Portland Art Museum. All these paintings were of artist friends and my family. All were full-length figures, head to foot. The paintings made use of large, flat areas of color, and not a lot of modulation in most areas, except in the faces. The example of Hockney's use of large flat background spaces was very much on my mind. All the canvases were the same size, 64"x48," most of them vertical. They were in acrylic, a medium I like for portraits, since it allows for a lot of correction and modification, without a thick buildup of surface. I found that the color became very rich when I applied many thin coats, laid over one another.

Doug Lynch designed a handsome four-fold brochure that reproduced all the paintings. (It was in black and white; affordable color printing was a few years off yet.) The show occupied the main gallery in the museum's balcony area, and the Oregonian did a two page spread on it.

Several portraits from that show, those of Bunce, McLarty, and the one of Mike Russo and Sally Haley, became part of the Art Museum's collection. Manuel's portrait was purchased for the State Capitol Building. The one of LaVerne Krause is in the collection of University of Oregon, where she taught for many years. The portrait of Portland Art Museum curator Rachael Griffin, was purchased by graphic designer Joe Erceg — to Rachael's chagrin. She had wanted to buy it, but had not spoken up until after Joe bought it. He wouldn't give it up, so I agreed to paint another one for her, one with a completely different composition. She liked that one quite well, and it later also went into the Museum's collection.

148

THE OREGONIAN, FRIDAY, FEBRUARY 11, 1977   4M   C11

SCENE FROM DANTE — Artist Jon Jelomon stands amid rubble of fire-ravaged gallery.

Work begun to salvage Fountain Gallery art

WHAT WAS LEFT — Occasional metal frames and only portions of paintings were all that fire left of hundreds of works.

SURVIVOR — This drawing, one of those that escaped destruction in Hughes Building fire, is carefully rolled.

WORK DAMAGED — Doll Gardner, wife of Portland artist Byron Gardner, examines some of husband's damaged work at new gallery location.

Staff photos by
MIKE LLOYD

By BETH FAGAN
of The Oregonian staff

A volunteer crew of some two dozen members of the Portland art community set to work Thursday to salvage what they could from the fire-ravaged Fountain Gallery.

Prowling the charred rubble in the gallery and its vast third floor storage area in the burned-out Hughes Building, they found blackened bronze and stone sculptures and several hundred water-logged drawings and prints which had escaped the four-alarm fire's path early Monday.

On the fourth floor, in a small room untouched by fire, some 40 of the 80 to 100 paintings which the gallery had stored for Portland artist Michele Russo

have been discovered.

Artists speculate the fire didn't reach the room because the freight elevator shaft which adjoins it had been walled off.

Another surprise discovery was a crate of paintings by local artists in the storage room. The paintings, most of them undamaged, had been stored for an art collector who moved to Alaska.

A partition had fallen on the crate and apparently protected it from the flames.

The large sculptures, by James Hanson, Frederic Littman, Hilda Morris and Tom Moranti, are scheduled to be hoisted from the building early Friday and returned to their makers for the long task of restoring patinas.

All other works salvaged from the rubble left by hundreds of destroyed paintings, prints, drawings and even ceramics, were being boxed and taken to the gallery's temporary quarters in the Tradewell Shopping Center at NW 21st Avenue and Davis Street. There, workers are sorting waterlogged works piece by piece and starting to dry them.

Material in artists' files, soaked with water but recovered along with slides of their work, also are being sorted piece by piece. Some of the records are all that remains of an artist's work.

The volunteers asked artists who had work in the burned gallery to drop by and see if any of their work that has been salvaged and appealed for others

who might be willing to assist in the salvage operation.

Along with the salvage crew, volunteers were helping with interior construction of the new gallery, which owner Arlene Schnitzer said she hopes to open within a month.

She said James Hanson, whose sculpture show had been scheduled to open last Wednesday, hopes to refinish his bronzes and show them. Only two were ruined by the fire.

For many volunteers, the salvage task was particularly sad. Jay Backstrand, examining badly damaged works from his show that had closed just before the fire, said he couldn't even talk about it.

Another volunteer, Denzil Hurlsey, left for several hours after his first trip into the burned gallery, but came back later. He said getting used to the idea of what the gallery had been and what it is now was too much for him to take in immediately.

In other developments since the fire, Peter Hero, executive director of the Oregon Arts Commission, said Thursday that the screening committee on art for the Oregon State Capitol had met and decided to seek new work by the same artists whose work, destined for the capitol, had been destroyed by the fire.

"The work chosen had really been the core of the collection being developed for the Capitol," Hero said. "Get-

ting new work from these artists will delay our schedule on installation, but we'll wait."

Mary Beebe, executive director of the Portland Center for the Visual Arts, said an informal meeting of people who are concerned about the impact of the fire on the art community will be held in the center at 6 p.m. Friday.

"It's hoped that something positive can come out of the disaster," Ms. Beebe said.

She said a meeting also is scheduled next Tuesday with Mayor Neil Goldschmidt.

She said one idea being discussed is the establishment of an endowment fund for a major permanent collection of Northwest art.

The Oregonian, Feb. 11, 1977

Fire

The big event of 1977 was the Fountain Gallery fire, which destroyed the gallery along with hundreds of artworks. The gallery was located on the second floor of a downtown Portland building. To keep warm, some vagrants had built a fire in the loading area. It got out of hand. Along with the gallery spaces, several large rooms stored a great many paintings and sculpture. I learned about the fire, and its destruction, early in the morning when I was on my way to Corvallis to give a talk about my work to a class at Oregon State University. The news reports on the car radio made it clear that the ongoing fire was consuming all the artwork there. Seventeen of my large, complicated paintings were among them.

Many of the slides I showed that morning were of those paintings. I didn't make a point of it in my talk, but as I projected the images, I was thinking to myself, "That one's gone. That one also. That one, too."

A few days later, I went to see the burned out gallery space. On a blackened wall hung the scorched remains of the stretcher bars of one of my paintings. It was one that I had based on a Muybridge photograph of a nude woman tossing a bucket of water. What pathos to think of the fire licking toward the painting and that nude figure pathetically throwing her bucket of water at it! Many years later, I did a close version of the painting from a slide. The fire didn't have the last laugh on that one, after all.

Teaching

During my long, 25-year tenure at the Museum Art School, I

"Ritual Gate-Smoke and Water," acrylic, 1975. Destroyed in the
Fountain Gallery fire, repainted 2006

taught painting, printmaking, and life drawing. What was called
second-year painting, was actually the first year that the students
got classes in painting. The philosophy of the school was that the
student needed a thorough grounding in the graphic skills of drawing, design, and composition before getting into painting. I think
for most of the students, this worked very well, though some were

chomping at the bit to paint long before their second year. I taught the second year painting for a number of years and enjoyed it a lot. There were so many fundamentals to teach, while at the same time, the students had the tools and skills to bring originality to the assignments. I spent many hours setting up still lifes, or devising setups for models, so as to bring out particular aspects of color and spacial relationships. The students were responsive, and it was like a compatible family, pushing along in the same direction, but with a variety of approaches. There was always a school exhibition at the end of the school year, held in the Art Museum. Bringing the best pieces together for that show was a happy time for everyone.

Life drawing was a requirement for all the students, for all four years. Since I do so much figure drawing myself, that was a natural subject for me to teach. To try to keep it fresh for the students, I often invented things to put on the model, or sometimes contraptions to put the model in. Often, suggesting different materials to draw with was useful, sometimes varying the pacing of the poses, sometimes drawing the figure very large, over life size.

Printmaking was another subject I loved teaching. I headed the printmaking department from 1965 to 1980, and taught intaglio printmaking. The students worked hard and produced strong prints. They were experimenting and pushing the limits. We did shaped plates, combined print mediums, used photo methods, and many other experimental methods that added to what the students had to say in their work.

Dean Givler was himself a very good printmaker, particularly in lithography. He had great enthusiasm for printmaking and gave it strong emphasis in the curriculum. It was one of the liveliest sections of the school, and many students adopted printmaking as their main medium of expression. And many of those, in turn, became teachers in other schools in the region.

A Sign from Heaven

I retired from teaching in 1980. I was only 52, but 25 years of teaching was a nice round number. Even though it was going to be a stretch financially, I felt that I had given it all I had, and in my classes, I heard myself repeat things I had said many times before. I wanted the extra time to spend in my studio. Teaching had given me a lot, in terms of clarifying my ideas and in the stimulation I got from the students. But not having to think about the students' work would allow me more concentration on what I wanted to do in my own painting.

As it happened, Mount St. Helens decided to blow its top off the week I retired. As I have remarked since, it was as if I had said, "God, if you think I should retire, give me a sign." And there it was. Plain as day.

The Picasso Show

In August of 1980, a huge retrospective Picasso show opened at the Museum of Modern Art. Manuel and I decided we had to see it. Phyllis didn't like long trips, nor the heat of New York summers. So Manuel and I set off for a ten-day trip to New York. But not before a lot of melodramatic prologue.

The morning of the flight, we were supposed to leave for the airport by 8 a.m. At 7:35 Manuel called me, and said, "The trip is off." He had had a big row with his then-girlfriend. They had been up all night arguing. Part of the argument was about why she couldn't go with us. There had been some pushing and shoving, and she had called the police. When they came, she declined to press any charges. But Manuel was very upset. At any rate, I said, "Look, we already have the tickets, and we've made our plans. We have to go." Luckily, Aaron was at home, and available to drive us. We jumped in our car, and picked up Manuel, and hustled toward the airport.

A few minutes later the girlfriend drew up alongside in her car, apparently determined that she was also going to New York. She was trying to pass us and looking straight ahead. Both of us were exceeding the speed limit. When we got to the airport, Manuel and I had the advantage of having a driver who could drop us off at the door, so we didn't have to park. The plane was to leave at a far gate in a couple of minutes. The ticket person called the boarding area, and we ran toward it with our carry-ons. There was no security check back then. They held the plane for us. We got on, and sat down, and anxiously watched the door until it closed. Whew!

Jackie and Cynthia

We had been invited to stay with Jackie Johnson and Cynthia Creasy, two former Museum Art School students, who had been living in New York for a few years. They shared the loft with a couple of others, who were away on vacation, so there was extra room. The loft was on the 5th floor, and a big, slow, freight elevator took us up. Jackie and Cynthia were both there to greet us. It was great to see them, particularly after the stressful start of the trip. Manuel was still frazzled. He eventually relaxed when he knew girlfriend was not going to find us.

August was suffocatingly hot, no air conditioning at the loft, and even at night it didn't cool off. There was access to the roof area, and on the roof at night there was some small respite from the heat.

The Museum of Modern Art was air-conditioned and the Picasso show was amazing. It took place on several floors, a vast retrospective. Manuel and I spent the whole first day on floor one, which covered only the first 20 years of Picasso's life and could have been a complete exhibition in itself. We spent three different days absorbing the rest of the show. We went to a free Lynda Ronstadt musical in Central Park. We played a lot of cards in the evenings. We rented a car for the four of us to make a day trip to Philadelphia. One evening we had dinner at a ground floor restaurant in the World Trade Center. Twenty-one years before it came down.

Manuel and I got a lot out of our New York trip, and once again Picasso worked his magic as a catalyst for me to stretch myself in my painting.

The Cat Lady

Both Phyllis and I love cats. We have had them ever since we were first married. At one point Aaron brought home an abandoned cat and her six kittens, which he found in an overturned box on his way home from school. That brought our household menagerie up to a total of ten cats. Eventually that number reduced itself through natural attrition, but we've always had at least one or two cats.

"Cat Lady," acrylic, 1976

Very early on, Phyllis got involved in doing something about the problem of pet overpopulation. With a local vet she formed the Responsible Pet Ownership Council, which sponsored spay and neuter programs. Later she helped found the Feral Cat Coalition. She was president of Animal Aid for a number of years, and also began and headed Friends of Shelter Animals. Our phone number was given out as the one to call with pet problems, and she spent countless hours patiently giving advice to anyone who called day or night. Over the years she was responsible for bettering the lives of literally thousands of animals.

Phyllis and me in our double scull, 2005

Chapter Eight

Rowing

Phyllis was always interested in trying new things. She had taken banjo lessons, got herself hypnotized in a class on self-hypnosis, and did some sessions with Toastmistress, becoming comfortable with public speaking, which served her well in her animal welfare work. She enrolled us in some folk dancing classes and also yoga sessions. Then when we were about 60, she talked me into taking lessons in single-scull rowing. Tom Leonardi was giving lessons to small groups at River Place Marina. It turned out to be a lot of fun, learning to balance the boat, maneuver it, and sometimes make it go fast. Tom was a good teacher. At one stage, the class went to the Y pool to learn to dump the boat over, and right it, and practice the techniques for getting back in it. (This worked very well in the nice warm Y pool, but a couple of years later when I unintentionally dumped over in the Willamette, it was a different story. More about that later.)

The next year we moved on to "Station L," a rowing club based on crew rowing. They gave (and still give) lessons, and there were enough students to form two or three eight-person shells. The experience of rowing the singles was very helpful, but "sweep rowing," as it is called when there are eight in the boat, is different in that you have only one oar, a long and heavy one, instead of two.

You have to be synchronized with all the other rowers. You row sometimes with a right-handed oar and sometimes left-handed. When practicing this skill, the four bow rowers steady the boat with oars held flat on the water, while the stern four row. The boat feels so tippy when you are first learning, it seems it will be impossible to balance when all the oars are rowing and off the water at once. Eventually, with experience, the rowers achieve balance and when the boat begins to move well, it feels like you are flying.

A Regatta

At the end of the first year of rowing in eights, a regatta was held for novices in Seattle on Green Lake, and we went there to participate. In the regatta, there were numerous races, and the boats had mixed crews, men and women. Aaron had also been taking lessons with us at Station L. He and Phyllis were in one boat together. I was in another boat in a different race.

Altogether, seven boats were on the starting line in my race. It is hard to describe the excitement, and the tension, sitting in an eight at the starting line. I was in the middle seat, number four. The boat is held at the starting place by a person on the float platform, and you are waiting for the command: "Ready, ROW!" You know that for the 1,000 yards of the course, you have to make your oar behave just right on every stroke. If your oar catches the water at the wrong angle ("catching a crab"), it fowls up the speed, and can even throw you out of the boat. You have to stay exactly with the beat the "stroke oar" sets, and you have to give it all your strength. There will be no possibility of saying, "I think I'm going to have a heart attack. Please stop for a minute."

Regatta, Green Lake, Seattle, WA, me far left, third boat from bottom, 1988

The boat I was in did pretty well. We came in fifth out of the seven shells. It felt good not to be last. The whole thing made you feel really alive! The stroke oar of Phyllis and Aaron's boat was Tiff Wood, an Olympic champion who lives in Portland, and was helping out that day just for fun. Even with an Olympic champion to set the stroke rate, the rowers were still novices, so it didn't make that much difference as to where they finished, but it did add to the excitement.

Phyllis and I rowed with Station L for a number of years. One of the requirements of rowing in eights is that, because most of the rowers have jobs that they need to get to later, the rowing needed to start really early, and we had to get up at 5 AM. In the winter, it was often dark when we launched the boat. The early hour had its difficulties, but I did find it very beautiful when sky and water were a saturated deep blue, from top to bottom. Plus the experience of seeing the landscape slowly, slowly emerge was a wonderful visual treat! I did quite a few paintings from the experience of those mornings.

Dumping Over

A couple of years later, Phyllis and I got together with a small group to row a four. These friends were about our age. They didn't need to get to jobs, so we were able to launch later in the morning. We didn't have to get up in the dark! We had some very pleasurable rowing sessions with that group. But on one occasion, a big wave from a passing barge tipped us over. It is a scary experience. Luckily we were near shore. Because our feet are secured in laced shoes in the boat, it can be tricky to quickly get out of them. Eldred, who was over 80, had his feet stuck briefly and there was an anxious moment while we helped hold his head above water and got him loose. This happened near the shore, right under the Morrison Bridge, with people crossing it, going to work. No one looked over the edge to notice our struggles to get the upside-down boat to the shore. I was reminded of the Bruegel painting of Icarus, his wings melted, falling into the sea while the farmer in the foreground paid no attention.

My Single

I rowed a single scull for several years. In rowing shells, you go without a life jacket, since wearing one would impede your

Me and my single scull, 1995

movement. One morning I was rowing along near the seawall. A
bunch of fishermen were lined up along the top of the wall with
their lines out, 15 feet above me. I was too near the wall and didn't
notice the fishing lines. The balance of the boat depends on each
oar being out to its side in unison. One of my oars caught a fishing
line, I was spilled into the water, and found myself suddenly looking up at the boat from underneath. I was surrounded by deep,
dark green color that got darker as it receded below me. All the
lessons we had learned at the Y flew out of my head. Instead of
moving the oars into a position parallel to the boat, so I could roll
it upright, I unscrewed them from the oarlocks. The boat floats,
since both hull ends are enclosed. But the seat well of the boat was

now full of water, and it took at least ten minutes of straddling the hull, trying carefully to screw the oars back into the oarlocks before I could get in without tipping back over. I was exhausted by the time I rowed it back to the dock.

I arrived home wet, and without my glasses and watch. For some time later, when we rowed past that spot on the river, I thought of my watch on the bottom, still keeping time, my glasses beside it, surveying the fishes.

John Booth and I rowed together in a double scull for several years. We would take the boat out from its berth at River Place, and row upstream, through the channel on the East side of Ross Island, to go up around the island and return. We went out a couple of times a week, rain or shine. One day, it started absolutely pouring, and we kept going, finally pausing near Ross Island Sand & Gravel's little boathouse on the shore of the channel. Some workers huddled there, waiting for the downpour to subside. They looked out at these two loony septuagenarians and shouted, "Are you having fun yet?" Actually, we were.

In a double scull, each rower has two oars, and the boat remains balanced, even though each rower may not be of equal strength. Phyllis and I owned our own double, and rowed it together a couple of times a week for many years. Eventually, it got hard for her to carry her end when lifting it off the rack and carrying it to the water. (It weighed about 45 lbs.) Also the balance needed to get in and out of the boat became an increasing issue for both of us. We rowed a couple of times a week until about 2010 when she was 85 and I was 82. I'm sure we were the oldest rowers on the river by the time we stopped rowing. We had rowed for about 23 years.

The Governor's Award for the Arts 1992

"Oh, my God," I said. Then I repeated it. I was at the kitchen table, opening the morning mail. Phyllis looked across at me, alarmed. Manuel had received the Governor's Award in 1991. I thought I might be considered for it sometime in the future, but I was completely surprised when I opened the letter to read that I was to receive the award for 1992.

Since it is a State of Oregon award, the ceremony takes place in different Oregon cities from one year to the next. This time, it was set for Newport, Oregon which has a handsome arts center to accommodate a large crowd. My sisters, Marianne and Carol and their husbands, and Phyllis, Aaron and my mother, were there. Don was there only in spirit, because he had an urgent assignation with a new love interest which took precedence at that time. Manuel was there, and a lot of other friends such as Ed and his wife Sandy from Los Angeles.

Ed, my cinematographer friend, brought his movie camera. The rules for the Governor's Awards ceremony apparently state that no outside recording is permitted. Somehow, with charm and brashness, Ed managed to set up his tripod and camera in the back of the hall, and got a nice recording of the proceedings. I think that those in charge couldn't quite figure out whether he had permission, or not.

Two of the other recipients that night were the composer, Tomas Svoboda and gallery owner, William Jamison.

Receiving such an honor gives you a chance to say a few things that have been your mind. I worked on my talk and it was a pleasure taking the podium and presenting it.

My Governor's Award Talk:

"When I think back on my first year at the Museum Art School, it doesn't seem to be a long time ago. I was 17 when I started at the Art School. I remember Bill Givler's composition classes, where we studied reproductions of the masters, to analyze how they made their wonderful paintings work.

And I remember my first day in Jack McLarty's life drawing class, waiting for the model to come out, and wondering if I might faint when she took off her robe to pose. I didn't. And I got used to it quite quickly.

My first painting teacher was Louie Bunce. He and I, and a couple of other students, would close up the local bar after night classes, two or three nights a week. We had endless discussions about art. Then there were Mike Russo's lively art history classes, where he made us see the effect of society on art, and vice versa.

A lot of art has happened since those days. My art and others. The thing that is sometimes overlooked about art is what a communal thing it is. We think of the artist alone in his studio with his struggles, and this is certainly part of the reality. But artists also work in conjunction with all the art that is being done by others. We do our work as part of a common language, and we test our work by showing it, and getting a reaction to it. We borrow ideas from each other. And in whatever way, great or small, each working artist contributes to the whole, marvelous language that is art.

And art thrives on encouragement. When I was a kid, the encouragement from my mother and father was vital to my growing interest in art. If we value what art does for our community, it deserves public, as well as private, support.

I want to thank my mother, Ellen, who is here tonight, and my father, who is here in spirit. And I want to take this opportunity to thank Pablo Picasso and Henri Matisse for all the help and inspiration they have given me over the years.

Thank you very much for this award. It will be a great incentive for me to press on, work hard, and make something of myself."

Newport, Oregon, 2-14-1992

Sculpture by Rick Bartow, the award I received at the
Governor's Arts Awards, 1992

The award itself is usually a work of art, commissioned for the
occasion, and presented to each recipient. (I did a limited edition
color etching, for the award in one of its first years). The award for
my year was a small sculptural carving by Rick Bartow. He did a
different carving for each award winner. It is a nice momento.

After the speeches, there was a presentation of dances by Native
Americans from the Siletz tribe. They invited the award recipients
up on the stage to dance along with them. We stomped our feet as
we followed them in a circle, around the stage. The tribe presented
each of us with a small piece of ceremonial bead work.

Friends and family stayed over in motels at the beach. We had
a big party in one of our motel rooms. And it was great to be able
to get out to walk on the beach the next day. The whole event was
a very happy occasion.

"Rain and the River," ceramic tile, The Portland Bullding, Portland, OR, 1988

Chapter Nine

Tile Murals

Around 1986, I began to experiment with ceramic tile, as a medium for making murals. The Percent for Art law was in effect, and there was lots of building and remodeling going on. All government projects were required to set aside one percent of the total budget to include artwork. Since there is a security issue with art that is placed in public spaces, it occurred to me that tile was an ideal medium, since it is relatively impervious to harm and therefore doesn't need special protection.

I had a difficult time trying to control the medium at first. I wanted to use it in a painterly way, with overpainting and refiring to get the color just right. When my friend, Connie Keiner, a ceramic artist, saw the first results, she said, "Why don't you just stick to painting?" But I am stubborn, and I had decided that I was going to conquer this medium. So I bought a kiln, and started making test tiles. Underglaze colors are very predictable if you control the firing time and temperature. I made hundreds of test tiles, keeping notes on each, and managed to gradually get the results I wanted. Some things I was doing were unorthodox because I didn't know that they couldn't be done. Because I didn't know that my methods weren't supposed to work, they somehow did.

Me working on "Mythscape: Day and Night", ceramic tile, 2007
Collection: Portland Community College, Rock Creek, Portland, Or

The Portland Building

The first tile mural commission I did was for the Portland Building in 1988. It covered the entire wall (8 x 10 feet) behind the receptionist's desk. It was an imaginative view of the West hills of Portland as seen from the river. Compositionally, I left a large, rather empty area, in the center of the image, to visually accommodate the receptionist. That worked quite well, I think. A couple of years later, the desk was moved to the other side of the room, leaving the mural more exposed. It worked even better without the receptionist!

Bremerton

Over the next decade that first tile work led to a number of

others in Portland, and elsewhere. One mural that was most interesting to do was for Bremerton High School in Washington State.
It is seven feet high and 32 feet long. I rearranged my studio to
have room to work on it. I couldn't see all of it at once, but I had
a very thorough color sketch to follow. When it was finished and
ready to take up to Bremerton, I decided I wanted to have it seen
in Portland first. I arranged with the Performing Arts Center to lay
it out on the lobby floor. Since a balcony overlooks the lobby, one
can get a good look at the entire 32-foot mural by looking down
from up there. It took several hours to lay it out on the marble
floor (being very careful not to drop, and break a tile). It was worth
the effort since a lot of people were able to view it, including a
contingent of students from the Art School.

    Tile murals are very portable until they are installed. This very

"Bremerton," ceramic tile, 1989, Bremerton High School, Bremerton, Wa

large tile work fit neatly into a couple of dozen cardboard boxes, and I was able to get the whole thing into my Volvo station wagon for transport to Bremerton. I hired a professional tile installer to put it up. Since it is located on the outside of the building, I wanted to be sure it was going to stay there with no possibility of it falling off sometime in the future.

Gun Shots

It took a couple of days to install it. Since the wall was of rough masonry, they needed to first attach metal screening to the wall, and then trowel on a flat platform of cement as a base for the tiles. When several rows of tiles were in place on the wall, some teachers came by and said, "Oh no. Not tile! This is a high school. It will never last!" Obviously, they were thinking about rival high schoolers who might throw rocks at it and shatter it to pieces. This concerned me somewhat, though I really knew better.

To reassure me, the installer took me downtown to show me a tavern with a front of decorative tile that he had put up some years before. "Here," he said, "Look at this." A couple of the tiles were sporting bullet holes. Somebody had been shooting at someone else outside the tavern. Small nickel-sized chunks had been taken out of the tiles. But nothing more. "And it was a big hand gun, probably a .38," he said. Tile backed by concrete, and supported evenly, is very strong. Even a hammer would only chip it, not cause crazing, or shattering. That was a relief.

The mural is on a South-facing exterior wall of the high school, and over the years I have wondered how well the color would hold up, given the weather and the mural's lengthy exposure to sun-

"Pool," ceramic tile, 2005, Peninsula Park Community Center, Portland, Or

light. After about 15 years, I visited it for the first time with some trepidation, wondering how much of it had changed over time. I had convinced myself that some of it must have faded, given that kind of ruthless exposure. To my great relief, all the color was unchanged. Even the delicate blues. Fired tile color is amazing. It's much more lightfast than oil or acrylic paints. Civics and history teachers sometimes take the students outside and use the mural to talk about the history of the region. I get a kick out of that!

Peninsula Park

My murals at Peninsula Park swimming pool are also open-air tile works. They consist of two four-foot by 20-foot murals flanking one side of the pool, and set into recessed spaces in the wall. The building is listed on the Historic Register, so my design had to pass not only the art committee, but also the Historic Preservation Committee. The best thing about that is that once approved and attached, my murals will be very hard to deaccession. A committee or an administrator in the future can't very easily say, "Let's scrape it off and try something else." They could, but it would be a very lengthy process to do that.

Peninsula Park is in a lower-income neighborhood, or it was at that time; things are changing rapidly in Portland. When I made the sketches for the mural, I took them to the site to show some of the art committee members. Kids were playing in the pool, and when they learned a work of art would be installed there, one of them said, "Oh boy, we get to have some art, too!" They had not seen what kind of art was being proposed. It was the idea of art itself, the idea that they were important enough to merit art.

The Portland Public Library Mural

Some of my ceramic murals are adhered to a framework of plywood, and are therefore portable. This is true of the six-by-nine foot, black and white tile work that is hung on the second floor of the Central Portland Library. Donated to the library by Brooks and Dorothy Cofield in 2007, it was one of several portable tile works I had done on my own, separate from the commissioned work. A very nice dedication ceremony was held when we unveiled it at the library. The Regional Arts and Culture Council sponsored the opening, and a number of my friends came. I worked out a cloth covering that could be pulled away, dramatically, by tugging on drawstrings. It was bright red, and when the strings were pulled, it did have the desired theatrical effect. I gave a talk, and I used an idea that my friend Joseph Mann had suggested, about pictures being the first books. I thought that worked nicely in the library setting.

One art form feeds another. For me, the ceramic tile pieces are an offshoot of my printmaking. There is something about the indirectness of both mediums that I am very much attracted to. In printmaking, you work on a plate, and then ink it, and pull the print, and that's the finished artwork. Tile work is done with colors that are paler, and sometimes quite different in appearance than the final result after the firing. In both cases, you do something in anticipation of something else. In the process, you are surprising yourself.

And in the case of black and white tile work, my method comes directly from the experience of making woodcuts. A black ceramic underglaze is applied to the white tile, and then the image is cut into it, exposing the white tile. I have always loved the quality of the black and white image. Sometimes it can get to the crux of experience more directly than color.

Symphony Drawings

In 1995, I started a series of oil-on-paper drawings of the Oregon Symphony. I have had a long-standing interest in music as a theme. There are all kinds of qualities that the visual and the aural arts have in common. Practically everything you can mention is a quality common to both — mood, color, texture, rhythm, pacing, detail, repetition. Also, I love to work with the shapes of person and instrument together.

Because Phyllis and I had season symphony tickets, I had plenty of opportunities to observe the players. I didn't want to disturb others by sketching during a performance, so I worked out a method of memorization. Since there was plenty of time to watch a pianist, for example, I would study the relationship between the player and the piano. Where did the feet go, where was the head in relation to the keyboard, how much of the left hand could I see compared to the right? Then I would close my eyes and draw it in my mind until I got to a place that was a blank. Then, eyes open, I would check on that part, close my eyes and start again, until I had it. When we got home, I immediately made a small sketch, as thoroughly as I could. The next day I started a full-size drawing, working from the small sketch. With practice, I got quite good at the process.

Equivalents

In 1999, I decided to do a millennium project. I set out to do some portraits of artist friends. They would be done in oil, on paper prepared with a coat of acrylic varnish, so that the oil doesn't soak in. Sections of the drawing could be erased with turpentine, or scraped out with the tip of a pallet knife. Each drawing involved only one dark color, sometimes black, sometimes an earth color, like burnt sienna. They are all brush drawings, with no added white. The finished piece sometimes looked like a charcoal drawing, sometimes like a more fluid brush drawing.

Bob Dozono was the first artist I asked to sit for me. In the past, I had worked from photographs when making a portrait.

"Equivalents," oil on paper, 2001, clockwise from upper left: Jack McLarty, Christine Bourdette, Manuel Izquierdo, Gordon Gilkey, Tom Hardy, Baba Wague Diakite, Lucinda Parker

Now I wanted to see what I could do with a sitter in front of me. I thought it would be helpful to limit each session to one hour, which would force me to make firm decisions and not get fussy. I also decided that the scale would be over life-size, so that I could really get involved with the planes and the relationship of one area to another. One other constraint was that I would leave something out in the drawing. I would not articulate everything.

The drawing of Bob seemed to come out well, and I liked what I got. I decided to do maybe a dozen of my artist friends. One thing led to another, and eventually it grew to be a very large group of drawings. When I contacted each artist, I asked them to sit for one hour. That was a time frame that worked better than asking them to give up a whole afternoon. I found that, because of the intensity of looking during that hour, I could work on the drawing later, even for a day or two, relying only on my visual memory.

Some people have stronger features than others and are easier to get hold of in drawing. I didn't know Rick Bartow very well and couldn't remember clearly what he looked like. When he knocked at my studio door at the appointed time, I opened it and said silently: "Thank you, God!" Bartow had wonderfully strong features, a strong hawk-like nose, and a mop of unruly hair, like a bird's nest. Good fodder for drawing.

The entire project was exciting — and demanding. I had to take a nap after each session. At times in the middle of the project, which lasted two years, I would ask myself "What are you doing? You're way out on a limb here." Then I'd realize it was okay; I just had to keep on going. I stopped when I reached 80 drawings. There was no way to include everyone. I knew I would be leaving out some good artists, but I had to stop somewhere.

In 2002, the Portland Art Museum mounted an exhibition, which included all 80 portraits. They produced a wonderful book for the show, which also reproduced all the drawings.

To quote myself from the book's introduction: "I've titled these drawings 'equivalents.' My aim is to produce a good drawing. The drawing may turn out to be a portrait in the sense that people may recognize the likeness of the subject in the drawing. But I am more interested in mining a presence, an essence of each sitter's character or spirit. If I can get that individual vitality of each sitter, the drawing becomes an equivalent of the person."

A Retrospective

In 2007, I was honored with a retrospective exhibition at the Hallie Ford Museum of Art in Salem, Oregon. That was an eye-opener. It gave me the chance to see my work, and therefore myself, in a kind of summarizing way. Roger Hull was responsible for curating the show, and the selection itself makes a statement about who George Johanson is. It was a very good grouping of my work, and covered about 60 years, during which I have worked in a number of different mediums and explored many different avenues. It started out with figurative art school work, followed by

Me, Roger Hull at my retrospective show, Hallie Ford Museum of Art, Willamette University, Salem, Oregon, 2007

Entrance to Rouffignac Cave, France

a section of abstract expressionist paintings. It moved on to figurative work involving invented environments, and then a section of
large scale portraits. Roger's choices pulled things together so the
show followed a consistent thread. I walked through the exhibit
alone, during one of the early days of the show, and said to myself,
"Well, I guess you really have done something, haven't you?" What
a nice gift I was given by my friend Roger Hull.

Paleolithic Art

One of my deep interests is in ice age art; in the question of
when, and why, early humans began to make pictures. As a picture

maker myself, I feel a direct affinity to those first artists. I feel that drawing, as such, was a breakthrough for the human race, and a huge boost to the further development of human consciousness. I have read every book I can find on the subject. And I have given several talks on "an artist's view" of the art of the caves and what the images might mean. One of my talks was presented to the Oregon Archeological Society, at the Oregon Museum of Science and Industry. The crowd was big, and it was exhilarating to give that talk to a group that already knew something about the subject, but not from the artist's point of view I was bringing to it.

In 2011, Phyllis, Don, and I went to stay with friends who lived in southern France, and we were able to visit some of the painted caves. One was a full-scale replica of Lascaux, (the actual cave is nearby, but can no longer be visited because of deterioration from mold, caused by so many visitors over the years). The replica is superb, exact in every detail, and it gives a wonderful sense of the original. Two of the other caves we visited are the actual caves, Pech Merle and Rouffignac, which, along with a dozen other art caves, are still open to the public.

Rouffignac is a cave that extends almost a mile into the hillside. A small, open, electric train takes visitors into the wide tunnel of the cave. One small light on the train is the only illumination. All the rest is pitch black. Rouffignac depicts more drawings of mammoths than any other cave, and it has many mammoth-bison combinations.

When we visited that cave it was off-season, and there were only five of us tourists on the train. The guide stopped about half-way into the cave, and he turned off the light. We were in intense blackness and silence. He stepped off the train, and about 15 feet

My sketch of the "Great Ceiling" at the cave of Rouffignac, France

away, he shone his flashlight on the wall. It appeared blank. Then he moved his light to the side, and in the raking sidelight, two mammoths appeared. Drawn by fingers in the soft clay of the wall, one had incorporated a small stone imbedded in the wall, as its eye. The mammoths were beautiful, and alive — and they were some 15,000 years old!

At the far end of the train ride, two-thirds of a mile into the dark, cold hillside, we came to a spot where we saw myriad drawings on "the Great Ceiling," an area 30 feet in diameter. There are over 60 animals drawn on this ceiling. It is utterly thrilling to gaze upward to see, just out of arm's reach, such beautiful drawings that look so fresh, and yet were done so many millennia ago. All are drawn with great sureness. Some look comparable to Picasso's expressive drawings of animals. All of them seem alive and vital.

Being inside the cave, deep in the earth, looking at those drawings, makes you sense the enormous time that has elapsed since they were done. And yet, here is the art, present right here with you, right now. Time collapses, and there is no interval at all between those first artists and us. Writing this memoir and looking back on nearly 90 years gives me something of the same feeling.

But life itself is all about time. Life is a big, beautiful, fantastic, messy train. It has been moving inexorably forward on its tracks for eons of time. You get on it. You do things. Eventually, you get off. The train keeps moving on as powerful and beautiful as ever, after you get off.

Maybe you left something of value on the train. You can hope so.

Afternotes

My art has gone through many phases. Whose hasn't, in 70 plus years of producing it? My student work was mainly figurative, with the strong influence of German Expressionism. Beckmann in particular was one of my favorite artists. (The Portland Art Museum owns one of his great paintings, "The Mill.")

My woodcuts and paintings, after my return from Mexico, got more abstract, but still incorporated the figure. Then for a period of five or six years I was heavily into abstract expressionism and any reference to figure or landscape was only hinted at. That was very liberating. The emphasis was totally on improvisation and a heavy build-up of paint. Dutch Boy white lead was available in five pound cans, and I used it liberally in my work. Those were heavy paintings. Bill Givler once asked me how many paintings I had done over the summer. I said, "I don't know exactly, but I used up about five cans of white lead."

Around 1962, I felt the need to return to the figure and started to do figures set in an abstract environment that was composed of mostly flat shapes. A rather alienated space for the figure to exist in. And the figures were somewhat generalized. Around the late 60s I began to ask myself, "Who are these people?" This led to a series of large complicated compositions that were based on

Photo for poster for my show at Sally Judd Gallery, Portland, 1972

photographs of family and friends. And often animals. We had a pet rabbit who had the run of the house and who became a strong presence in several paintings. As did a pet jay and many cats.

Travels to Greece led to a series of take-offs on Greek myths. Then there was a series of large, full-length portraits.

Mural commissions in the percent-for-art program followed. These often involved historic research, which I enjoy very much since it leads to subject matter that I would not otherwise think of doing.

Exploring and using different materials has been a longstanding interest of mine. My murals are often done in ceramic tile. I have also explored sculpture, using plywood in some and cut out aluminum shapes in others. These sculptures are very much related to the figurative shapes I use in painting. And of course I have used many different materials and approaches in my printmaking. Printmaking in all mediums is something I have done all my life, along with painting.

Colored Grounds

I often begin a painting with arbitrary colors as a ground. I find it more interesting than beginning on a blank white surface.

On one particular canvas, I was assisted by my granddaughter Sonja. She was about four, and she loved to paint. On a piece of paper, she would start out with fresh, clear colors, and then delight in gradually stirring them all into a rich, brown mud. It was interesting mud, but it ended up being mostly a mud pie.

As an experiment, I decided I would have Sonja do the colored ground for a large painting I was about to start. So I gave her about six different acrylic colors to work with, and had her just go to town on it. The canvas was 60x40, and she had a good time covering the whole surface. No image, just a lot of color. I stopped her before the mud pie stage. I used what she had done as the ground color for my painting, and kept as much of her under-color as I could in developing the painting. Sonja's color made a nice contribution to the finished work. I later sold the work, and the buyers were enthralled with the story behind its beginnings. I should have had her start more canvases for me.

When I'm painting, the work is always speaking back to me. And sometimes the painting takes off and goes somewhere I hadn't intended, all on its own. At other times, in a good way, the painting paints itself. Conscious choices are set aside, and some other entity seems to be doing the work.

No one knows what art is. Though many thousands of words have been written about it, art can never be entirely defined. What is true, however, is that art is of special importance to our humanity and has revealed a very great deal about who we are as human beings.

"In The Studio," oil and acrylic, 2015

Subject Matter

My art revolves around a number of subjects and themes. A couple of years ago, I made a list, just for my own edification. Here is the list as I wrote it down:

>Bathers
>
>Rowers
>
>Swimming Pools
>
>Portland Landscape — Volcanoes
>
>Night Amusement Parks
>
>Cave Art — Myth — History
>
>Crowds — Umbrellas
>
>Self Portraits — Personal Myth
>
>Cats — Dogs
>
>Music — Jazz — Dance
>
>Portraits
>
>The Studio

I Love:

Nocturnal light.

The drama of contrasts.

The double image, where a shape has more than one meaning.

How a thing is made, along with the thing itself.

The almost audible sound of pure colors.

Exploratory, searching drawing.

Expressive, messy drawing.

The freedom and irresponsibility of beginnings.

Biography

George Johanson graduated from the Museum Art School in Portland, Oregon in 1950 with further study in New York and London. He taught at the Museum Art School (now the Pacific Northwest College of Art) for 25 years until his retirement in 1980. He has had more than 60 solo exhibitions and is represented in public and private collections, including the Portland Art Museum, the Hallie Ford Museum of Art, Salem, Oregon, the National Collection of the Smithsonian in Washington, D.C. and the Victoria and Albert Museum, London.

In 1992, Johanson received the Oregon Governor's Arts Award. He was given a 60-year retrospective of his work at the Hallie Ford Museum, Salem, Oregon in 2007.

He maintains a studio in Portland and continues to exhibit actively.